Animal Communication—Our Sacred Connection

Animal Communication— Our Sacred Connection

Jacquelin Smith

2005

Galde Press, Inc.

Lakeville, Minnesota, U.S.A.

Animal Communication—Our Sacred Connection

© Copyright 2005 by Jacquelin Smith

All rights reserved.

Printed in the United States of America

No part of this book may be used or reproduced in any manner whatsoever without written permission from the publisher except in the case of brief quotations embodied in critical articles and reviews.

First Edition

Second Printing, 2006

Cover photograph by Allie Kattoua

Jacquelin Smith with Skye and Serrie

The poem, "The Visitor," previously appeared in *Species Link.*

Library of Congress Cataloging-in-Publication Data

Smith, Jacquelin
Animal communication : our sacred connection / Jacquelin Smith.
p. cm.
ISBN 1-931942-24-2 (trade pbk)
1. Human-animal communication. 2. Telepathy. I. Title.
QL776.S62 2005
133.8'9--dc22

2005026233

Galde Press, Inc.

PO Box 460

Lakeville, Minnesota 55044–0460

This book is dedicated to Chloe, Etheria, and Bella. They were my beloved friends and teachers who enriched my life in countless ways.
Thanks for teaching me how to soar.

Contents

Acknowledgements

I thank my dear friend, and confidante, Connie Parkinson, for the great job you did in editing. Thank you for your love, support, and for the faith you had in this book from the beginning. I thank my good friend, Fred Andrle, for your support, love, and the wonderful job in helping edit. Also, thank you Lynda Sowers for your encouragement and support and input as a friend during the final rewrite. Thank you M. J. Abell for your friendship, your creative ideas, and computer knowledge. Also, thanks to Phyllis Galde and the staff at Galde Press for their guidance and belief in this book.

I thank all the animals, people, and other living beings for their insight, wisdom, and stories which made it possible to write *Animal Communication—Our Sacred Connection.*

I thank everyone, in every realm, who guided me on the journey of writing this book.

Teach Us

Teach us God to listen to our spirit
To be kind to every living being
To walk in harmony and joy each day
To let the love in our hearts lead the way.

—Jacquelin Smith

Foreword

We are living in an age of change; serious, capital C Change. People everywhere are being challenged by the opening of new paradigms of expression. In fact, animal communication is not really a new expression; spiritually aware people have been doing this for centuries, but an acceptance of this unique gift is only now beginning to percolate into the greater human awareness.

I am therefore delighted when a person like Jacquelin Smith writes a book that is as approachable and informative as *Animal Communication—Our Sacred Connection*. I confess, I smiled when I read about her attempts to validate this gift to rather skeptical people. I have learned that where there is openness validation is not necessary, while a closed mind will accept none. This book, however, is one of the most validating books that you could read to affirm that yes, your own inner experiences of animal communication are most probably real.

A number of years ago I was approached by a farmer with a thousand acres, five thousand sheep, and a few sheepdogs. His problem was the dogs. They were chained when they were not working and barked their protest nonstop day and night. He had tried everything to stop this. If the dogs were loose, they either wandered far away or continuously worked the sheep. I asked him if the dogs had been educated. "Yes, they've been trained," he replied. I shook my head. "Not trained, educated." He looked bemused. "Have you ever told the dogs clearly and precisely how you want them to behave?" I asked. He laughed. "Mate, they're just bloody dogs."

"Wrong," I told him, and went on to explain that most dogs are remarkably intelligent, but they very seldom receive clear communication from their owners. I suggested that when his mind was clear and uncluttered, that he take the dogs for a walk right around the boundary of his farm, all the time focused on, and clearly telling his dogs, that this is the boundary and that they are not to stray beyond it. The next step is to walk among the sheep clearly communicating that the sheep are only to be worked by the dogs on your command. You then tell the dogs that they will no longer be chained when not working.

He looked at me as though I was mad, muttering that he might give it a go. Six weeks later I received a letter from him. It had taken him two weeks to get in a really clear, nonskeptical state of mind, and then he had done as I suggested. He said that to his and his wife's total astonishment and delight the dogs had done exactly as he had told them. They no longer barked, strayed, or bothered the sheep.

Jacquelin's wonderful book is full of stories like this, covering a very wide scale of working in cooperation with Nature and of communicating with animals. As you read though these pages you will soon realize that it is not the animals that have to learn the skills of communication, it is us. We have become so separated from Nature, so lost to the greater reality that all life is the expression of One consciousness, that we have not only forgotten how to communicate with Nature, we also have serious problems in communicating with each other. Read this book, I thoroughly recommend it. But don't just read the words. Read it, feel into it, connect with the consciousness of the book, learn...and then apply what you learn into your life. Both you and Nature will benefit.

—Michael J. Roads

Author: *Talking with Nature/Journey into Nature; Getting There,* a novel; *The Magic Formula; More than Money: True Prosperity*

Chapter One

Unfoldment

I GREW UP with dogs, alligators, turtles, snakes, and a friendly black crow, among others, and have always cared deeply about animals.

I have always been intuitive, often knowing what was going to happen ahead of time and picking up images and feelings from people and objects. This led to an active study of metaphysics at age eighteen.

My study of animal life and behavior began in 1972. I also pursued courses in psychology to better understand animals. After obtaining my animal technician's license, I proceeded to work in that field. Then, in 1977, I was involved in a serious car accident that changed my life and caused me to have a near-death experience. After the accident, I was forced to leave my position because I could not physically function the same as previously.

After the accident, I began studying various aspects of ESP (extrasensory perception) in more depth. Within a few months of practicing meditation, I experienced an incredible outflow of many and varied psychic skills. I felt as if the floodgates of a dam had been opened and knew the accident had altered my path. Intuition had always been flowing for me, but meditation and the near-death experience allowed these abilities to emerge in a bigger way. As my knowledge and experience in using these natural intuitive skills grew, I offered my consulting services to people concerning personal issues.

During this time I began an apprenticeship with a woman who was highly respected for her dog training and behavioral work in Ohio. I began guiding friends' dogs through her courses, then branched out on my own.

I started wondering if there was a way to combine my love for animals with my intuition. Then an idea hit me: If telepathic communication exists between people, why not between humans and animals? So I decided to try and communicate telepathically with an animal.

In this book, I will use fictional names to protect my clients and the animals.

MY FIRST EXPERIENCE was in 1979 with a male lowland gorilla at a zoo. I had an acquaintance who worked there and could verify any impressions I might see, hear, or feel. I didn't know what to expect. The first time I visited with this gorilla, I was astounded by the many images and thoughts that appeared to me. Like a movie within my mind, I saw a young gorilla in the wild romping through green vegetation with other gorillas. Suddenly the scene and feelings shifted. I could see and feel his pain of being taken from his mother in Africa. The mother was killed! This used to be a common practice in order to capture a young wild gorilla. I saw him in a small cage on a boat and could feel the rocking motion of ocean waves.

A person who worked at the zoo verified these facts, for I had not known he was captured from the wild nor that he was transported in a crate.I felt this gorilla's frustration and unhappiness about those old, frightening experiences as well as his dissatisfaction at existing in his present cage at the zoo. Today most zoo animals are born in captivity, so there is no painful remembrance of being kidnapped from the wild. Within a short time, I was able to ask him questions and receive his thoughts, as well as know his feelings. He told me, "The memories of humans killing my mother and pushing me into a crate lived within my cells, within my memory. They are still here. Certain situations make me feel the same way I did then." This gorilla now lives in a natural habitat and is much happier.

I WAS ECSTATIC TO LEARN that it was possible to leap beyond the boundary of the physical form of an animal and to communicate with his or her personality and spirit.

Soon, I became aware how this connection was possible. The common denominator is life itself. The life force exists in all forms of life, and is, therefore, the common link between us. If I am in touch with my spark of life then I can consciously connect with another's spark and know them.

An exchange can take place. This is what allowed me to know the experiences and feelings of the lowland gorilla. It is the most direct and intimate way of communicating with an animal.

This connection is not paranormal or psychic. We usually think of intuition as something outside of us, but intuition means being taught from within. An example of telepathic communication is the common experience of calling someone on the telephone only to hear them say, "I was just thinking about you." We send and receive each other's telepathic messages every day, but seldom make any conscious effort to acknowledge or develop what are natural abilities.

I knew that thoughts were energies. This is how we are able to pick up on each other's thoughts even though we are not usually aware of this process. Learning how to send clear, direct messages enables an animal to know our thoughts and intentions with clarity.

Also, I learned through experience that whatever thoughts or images I sent to or received from an animal were communicated in ways we both understood. Being human, I receive images, words, thoughts, and feelings. Animals can perceive whatever images I send, since this is the primary perception between us. Animals also feel the intention of the energy being sent to them. Behind each word or image is an energy or vibration that our spirits naturally understand. The vibration, or the intention, behind the word is translated in ways that the animal and I will understand.

Here is an example showing the power of thought. My cockatiel companion, Etheria, had escaped from my house and had flown into high treetops across the street. She did not know how to come down, so I decided to try to telepathically bring her to me. I sent out energy-packed images of her flying to me. But first I had to get her attention telepathically because she was busy eating leaves. I asked her to concentrate on my images, and within ten minutes she started flying above the tree. My mistake was that I did not stand far enough away from the tree's branches for her to see me. She flew around the tree several times and ended up landing back on the top branches. Then she was too scared to fly again. But by the next day, she had flown down to the lower branches and I was able to put her in her cage.

I also began to realize that whenever I would focus my attention to a particular spot in a room that I was in, my companion cat, Chloe, would go and sit there. This again convinced me just how real energy is and that she could perceive it when I would focus and set my intention.

Communication

I BEGAN COMMUNICATING TELEPATHICALLY with many zoo and domestic animals. I communicated with chickens, dolphins, bats, snakes, horses, cats, dogs, spiders, lions, birds, and many other magnificent species. I started keeping a journal of communications with animals, which I still record.

Years later, I spent numerous hours observing the behavior of captive animals in zoological parks. Also, I traveled to Kenya and Rwanda in Africa to observe animals in their natural habitat. I had the opportunity to sit among and communicate with mountain gorillas, whose numbers have dwindled significantly. Also, I had the opportunity to observe and communicate with animals in areas of South America, including the Galapagos Islands.

Through experience, I learned that each animal communicates differently. Some animals are serious, while others are humorous. Some are scattered in the way they communicate, while others are focused and thoughtful. An animal's unique personality is reflected through his or her distinctive style of communicating. It is reflected through the words, feelings and images that I receive from them. It is always amazing and fun getting to know the animals.

I discovered that it was possible to communicate with the personality as well as the soul of an animal. Sometimes the personality's wants differ from the soul's desires. I communicate with the different aspects of the animal's Self. In doing this, it gives a more balanced picture of what is going on with the "whole" animal.

As I continued on my journey, I learned that it was possible to understand the consciousness of any species by connecting with an animal of that particular species.

In continuing to sharpen my skills as an animal communicator, I felt I should have a business name and decided on "Species Connection." I began offering my services of communicating with animals throughout the country.

Distance is no problem in telepathic communication work. Most people have experienced this at some time. Again, think of the example of calling someone and hearing them say, "I was just thinking about you."

I began giving lectures and offering workshops on interspecies communication and holistic health with animals. This opened the way for me to be a featured guest on TV, local and national radio talk shows, as well as giving interviews for newspaper and magazine articles.

Validation

I ALWAYS LOOK FOR A WAY TO VALIDATE my work if possible. A zoo research director and I worked together to validate some of my findings. Once he asked me to tell him about a problem with a particular leopard about which only he knew. When I said,"This leopard is having eye problems," he laughed and said,"Yes, she is." But it was difficult to fit these findings into a scientifically acceptable form. For a number of years I was determined to prove the validity of my work. I visited one professor at a major university to see if he could be of assistance. He asked me to tell him about his dog. I mentioned some general characteristics that someone could have guessed, but then told him in specific terms about his dog's back problem and how he had great trouble getting up and down the stairs. His response was,"How did you know that? Have you talked to my wife or children?" I didn't know his wife or children. I had proven that telepathic communication is real, yet he refused to consider the possibility. When I saw him a month later he was still asking how I knew about his dog's back problems.

I then approached several animal psychologists to work on a project to validate my work. There were many problems with trying to fit intuition into a scientific framework. After a year of work they informed me that they did not know how to measure and correlate all the information.

There were so many hidden variables that might never come to light by using this process. I would sense and receive specific information from the animal, but often the animals' people did not observe, know, or remember things about their animal companions. One dog communicated telepathically to me that he was very uneasy around fire. His person said he wasn't aware of this being true. I mentioned this to the dog trainer who had sold this man his dog. The trainer was silent for a moment and then said,"When that puppy was a few weeks old there was a fire in his kennel and that pup almost died."

I finally resigned myself to the fact that trying to prove that telepathic communication exists between humans and animals wasn't going to work. Yet today, intuition and science are finding a common ground on which to validate such findings.

The more experiences that took place between the animals and myself, the more validation I received from people and the Universe, which allowed me to develop a stronger trust in interspecies communication work.

My knowledge and many of my discoveries are based on over twenty-five years of experience in communicating with thousands of animals.

I am happy to say that the animals taught me how to communicate with them telepathically.

Opening to Animals

IN OPENING COMMUNICATION CHANNELS with animals, not only did I sense the love, joy, and wisdom from an animal, but if there was pain or suffering, I would sense or receive images of that, too. After my cat companion, Bella, had been with me for five years, I began sensing that she was in pain with headaches, and then she began to lose her balance on window ledges.

I had fallen in love with Bella the first time I saw her at Cat Welfare. The welfare volunteer said to me, "A university student dropped her off and said she's been used experimentally. Usually they sacrifice [kill] them, but he couldn't bear to do it to her."

So I took her home. As I was just beginning to learn about how to communicate, she showed me the horrors and suffering she had been through. Her life ended at age five due to tests that had been performed on her. She had developed a rare neurological problem. She was one of the most loving animals I have known. My friends who had never liked cats loved her. She transformed any old beliefs they had about cats.

TELEPATHIC COMMUNICATION is a heart-to-heart language that all living forms know and understand. It is a profound spiritual connection. What we humans call intellect cannot be used to communicate with other forms of life. This heart-to-heart exchange is beyond words because it is a nonverbal, nonlinear experience. Trying to put it into words is like trying to experience love through words. It can't be done.

As time went on, I learned it was possible to experience a loving, sharing relationship with all forms of life. I learn more every day, and I admire and have great respect for all life forms, from the slugs who creep along on wet leaves to those powerful lions who prowl the savannahs of Africa. We are all different but equally significant expressions of the Creator. Every life form offers unique qualities that enrich and create the whole of life on Earth.

One day, while dancing through the ocean's waves, I suddenly experienced being *one* with everything. I was the water, the sky, the sand, the seagulls, and the burning orange sunset.

THE MORE EXPERIENCE I GAINED in consulting with people's animals, the more my eyes were opened to the great extent humans affect their companion animals. It's not unusual for me to spend an equal or greater amount of time consulting with the human about their animal's problem. This is especially true if the animal's behavior is directly tied to their person's attitudes and issues.

Today, as an animal communicator, I offer a blend of telepathic communication skills as well as traditional and holistic ways to deal with all kinds of issues.

Before doing a consult, if I feel there might be a medical problem, I always make sure the animal has been checked over by a veterinarian. A physical problem can develop from emotional issues.

In this book I talk about my experiences which go beyond any belief systems. In fact, many of my encounters with animals and other life forms have shattered ideas I thought I had learned.

Animals have taught me how to see within them. They were and are my teachers. I have had to leave old definitions and linear categorizations about various species behind in order to experience and learn from animals.

This book is about much more than interspecies communication. It is about learning that other life forms have purposes that are as important as our own. We can experience the important universal connections between all life forms. The animals know us well; let's take the opportunity to know them better.

In order to achieve clear communication in this book, I use "animal" as though it does not also refer to the human animal. I have also chosen to refer to animals as "he" or "she" because animals are not "its."

My intention in writing this book is for all of us to expand our way of thinking about and relating with animals. In a number of chapters I offer practical ways to enhance close ties with animal companions.

Hopefully, this book represents a wholistic attitude and awareness so we can see how we affect animal friends and how we can enhance our relationships. And since all life forms are interconnected, it's important to care about the whole of Nature and the Earth.

IN JANUARY 1998, I started the Divine Prayer Line for Animals. The purpose of the prayer line is to pray for those animals who need assistance for all kinds of problems. I mail out a quarterly newsletter to members. There is a group of us who get together and pray for specific animals, as well as various species, animal organizations, and many others, including the Earth in an effort to spiritually support all living beings. We continue to see many miracles happen.

Terms

SOME OF THE IDEAS AND TERMS that I use in this book are based on my experiences in movement awareness work, meditation, shamanism, and various other areas of work with intuition.

"Centered" is an inner feeling, experience that allows a person to establish a sense of peace and calm from which to communicate. Physically speaking, this energy center is just below the belly button. By connecting to our inner center, we can direct our energies in the way we truly wish to. Being centered enables us to open and move with and through changes, going beyond conditioning.

Being "grounded" is feeling connected and solid in relationship to ourselves and the Earth. This is done by allowing any busy thoughts and energies to flow down our body and into the Earth by creating a tube of light that flows from the tailbone or root chakra deep into the Earth. It helps to feel our feet firmly planted on the ground. This helps us establish a solid connection with ourselves as a preparation for directing energies with interspecies communication or life in general.

See Within an Animal

THERE'S ALWAYS MORE THAN MEETS THE EYE in relationships with those animals we care about the most.

Animals have reasons for everything they do, and are trying to give us their messages. Their behavior can be misinterpreted, and this is where telepathic communication helps to bring clarity. The best way to know what your animal friend is experiencing is to ask him or her.

Everyone has a natural ability to communicate with animals and other life forms. We can see within an animal rather than just the physical form. First, we must learn how to experience an inner quiet. Then we will we be able to see and hear the animals who are so willing to communicate about themselves.

THIS BOOK IS WRITTEN not only for those people who are interested in learning how to communicate with animals, but also for those people who are interested in strengthening the bond with their own animal companions.

I am delighted to share some of my personal experiences and the knowledge I've gained in communicating with the animals since 1979. As you read, accept what feels true for you and set aside what does not seem true for you. Trust your own intuition.

My hope is that others will use their natural intuitive abilities to experience the joy of carrying on conversations with animals and to celebrate the oneness of Nature and of all life.

Chapter Two

Our Separation and Oneness with Nature

Come out into the light of things,
Let Nature be your teacher...
Come forth, and bring with you a heart
That watches and receives.

—Wordsworth
"The Tables Turned," 1798

BEFORE LEARNING how to communicate with animals, it's important to first understand our fundamental connections with Nature, and how we humans, in many ways, have separated from Nature.

Millions of years ago the human animal intuitively knew itself, like other forms of life, to be a part of Nature. We resided with all of Nature's diverse beings. All life forms played an equally important part since they actually *were* the environment. The various life expressions communicated nonverbally. Humans listened to and followed their spontaneous, wordless intuition of mind, body, feelings, and spirit. We knew our primordial roots were in Nature. We could directly experience the rhythms of the moon and sea. We could directly experience animals and other life forms.

Humans wading through a stream could experience being the stream's essence, yet retain their own identity. All forms of life could directly experience, learn from, and know each other. These were deep ties and friendships between species. All life forms experienced being one, and therefore knew how to co-exist. We could say that this was the Garden of Eden. This was before the mind/ego of humans took over and before humans made poor choices about how to use their power.

The life force that still flows through all living beings is what links us together today, creating this oneness. Open channels of consciousness flow from, and through, all life forms. These are the energy connections that allow all forms of life to attune themselves naturally to one another's unique inner rhythm. It's through these channels that knowing and communicating nonverbally happens in a direct way.

THE CONCEPT OF THE WHEEL beautifully illustrates our connections with one another. Let's say the wheel represents our Universe. The center or hub of the wheel is the energy force that gives us all the gift of life. There are numerous spokes that extend from the hub. Each spoke is a species that lives on Earth. Each spoke plays an important part so the wheel functions as a balanced, flowing system. Each spoke is then fastened to the rim. The rim is the thread of energy that connects all forms of life. It's the rim's connections that allows the wheel to move as a working whole with natural cyclings. Without the various spokes interlocking with the rim, there would be no wheel.

It is also true if enough of the spokes are destroyed, there are wobbles which eventually lead to total breakdown and collapse. Therefore, every spoke is of equal importance! The entire system must have all its spokes for it to be a smooth-rolling wheel.

Language

AS THE INTELLECT AND VERBAL LANGUAGE EVOLVED, humans forgot about their intuition and connection with other life forms. Nonverbal language, which is nonlinear, was set aside as we focused on linear speech. Our minds became cluttered by constant thinking in words, which cut us off from our intuitive flow. Consciousness was now considered to be contained within the mind. As a result, we stopped feeling our conscious connection with life forms through direct, spontaneous experience that extended beyond the boundaries of the body.

Language of speech became a god. Intellect, speech, and written language are wonderful abilities, but it's the way humans focus on and overemphasize them that causes us to deny other natural abilities that are equally important.

Separation from Nature

THIS IMBALANCE WITHIN THE SELF separates us from direct experience within ourselves and with other animals. It creates a split within ourselves.

Our mind emphasizes separating everything and everyone into categories, but spiritual oneness with Nature transcends the mind.

Before the mind became the main focal point for consciousness, the mind, body, emotions, and spirit flowed in a unified way. Today our minds control our thoughts and feelings, often creating inner struggles.

As humans physically and spiritually separated from Nature, we no longer felt a kinship with Nature, but started fearing her.

As the human species multiplied and began to take control, possessing other animals and forms of life, the environment became unbalanced. Agriculture played a key role in separating humans from Nature. As agriculture developed, various animals, when domesticated, became subject to the imbalance of human culture. Domestic animals were considered good since they were resources to help us with tasks and as food. Other animals who were thought of as nuisances or predators were now adversaries. People began killing the wild animals who destroyed their crops and domestic animals. War was declared against Nature.

Animals no longer truly benefited from being in a relationship with humans. Mutual respect and give-and-take were gone. What other animals wanted or needed was no longer important to human beings.

Villages and cities arose and civilization grew and spread out on the land. Humans became even more separated from Nature, both physically and spiritually.

Most people no longer saw wild animals, but those who did told tales. Often the stories were spun from projections of their own traits onto the animal.

Many animals became scapegoats for what we wouldn't accept as part of our own Nature. Desirable qualities of animals were incorporated into the variety of beliefs. People believed the tales, passing them on to their children, friends, and neighbors. We still do this today. This is how folklore and myths about animals have been passed down through time. People saw animals as symbols that represented various attributes, containing emotional charges, rather than being seen for themselves as whole beings.

For example, one animal that was unfairly maligned for more than two thousand years all over the world is the wolf. Many cultures have projected malicious and evil qualities onto the wolf. One of the most common beliefs was that they were vicious and bloodthirsty. In Europe, the folklore of werewolves, man turning into a wolf during full moon, terrified people. Wolves were exterminated in great numbers because of such myths. Today, we know wolves aren't vicious or bloodthirsty. In fact, wolves and humans live in very similar social systems.

False beliefs about animals that emerged from myths are reflected through our language in terms like beast, weasel, snake, pig, rat, dumb ass, bird brain. These are used in derogatory ways to describe human beings.

We use traits that we would like to possess to describe ourselves or others. For example, strong as a tiger, quick like a bunny, sleek as a cat, happy as a lark.

Our beliefs have also been shaped by the way animals are portrayed in cartoons, films, and fairy tales.

What about "Little Red Riding Hood" or the "Three Little Pigs"? They appear as harmless tales, yet can influence our perception of animals while young.

Gorillas are shown as aggressive beasts who attack humans. King Kong is a violent monster who lusts after Fay Wray. In reality, gorillas are gentle, shy vegetarians.

Night creatures are thought of as evil. This has to do with our distorted idea that darkness is evil and that light is good. Bats are labeled vicious, repulsive creatures who are ready to swoop out of the night skies to entangle themselves in young girls' hair.

Hunters who killed for sport often twisted the truth about encounters with animals and uncivilized Nature to make themselves appear as courageous heroes. Their remarks about animals greatly contributed to peoples' false beliefs about various animals in the wild.

The early church played a part in distorting peoples' views about Nature by declaring animals to be soulless, depraved, lowly beasts to be dominated by man. Man himself was said to have the same beastly, sinful Nature as the lower animals, and was required to control this evil Nature. This only drove humans further away from Nature and themselves.

Most people blindly accepted and followed these teachings as truth.

AS SCIENCE ENTERED the scene, it was viewed as a god. Yet science's way of pursuing knowledge by using "objectivity" created a deeper division between humans and the rest of life. The supposedly objective standards and methods developed by science were subjective. This is because they were produced by humans who built their methods on ages of subjective human attitudes, bias, and prejudice about the world. Humans, since they developed a language of symbols, were assumed to be the most superior life form and the only being who could think and reason. Of course, this was from the humans' point of view.

In science's efforts to understand Nature, it focused on outward form, often scrutinizing the dead form to discover what made it tick. The form was dissected into parts and categorized as if this could uncover the secret of life.

It makes more sense to learn about life from the living. And even then, it's still easy to project our human prejudices onto the animals and their behaviors.

The life force, or spirit, that creates life is not included as a part of the scientific method but disregarded. This blinds us to seeing who the animals truly are as "whole" beings.

To watch animals in their natural environment and to be in relationship with them is the most direct way to learn about them and to understand how they grow, develop, and live their lives.

It is the intelligible, universal spark of life flowing through all animals and other life forms that allows us to know intimately who they truly are.

In looking at Nature's amazing creations as distant from and less than humans for many centuries, we've lost perspective of our interrelatedness with all life. We end up seeing in a distorted way only what fits into our beliefs about what Nature is supposed to be. Unfortunately, many feel we have overcome primitive ways and that we are independent from Nature. We humans forget that all beings are dependent on each other in some way. In abandoning Nature, we abandon ourselves.

Price of Civilization

Many people believe that we are unrelated to Nature and have left it behind. We deeply feel the effects from this unbalanced view and way of life. We seldom listen to the rhythm of Mother Earth, feel the change of tides, gaze into a star-filled sky, or look into the moon's face.

Problems people cope with in our society often stem from this unbalanced way of life. This explains why we feel alienated from others and from ourselves. We feel fragmented in the midst of concrete, glass, and metal. Our being out of touch with both outer and inner Nature leaves us feeling unfulfilled, as if something's always missing. These are spiritual needs that can be filled by connecting with the divinity within ourselves, the Creator, and the rest of creation. Connecting with the animals, trees, sky, and the Earth brings us back to our wholeness and balance.

Since we have been apart from Nature for so many generations, many of our natural senses have become dim and repressed. To awaken and use these senses is to remember who we—and other life forms—truly are.

We intuit these imbalances in our spirit because people are consciously and unconsciously attempting to reconnect with Nature.

We have been taught in our society that the spirit is less important to care for than the body. We divide ourselves up into parts—mind, body, emotions, and spirit. In dividing mind and body how can we know what we feel? We no longer function as integrated, whole beings.

Why is it people feel so much better when they make time to walk in the woods or camp in a park? On some level, we are remembering our connections with Nature, with our source and our wholeness.

Reconnecting with Nature

WE CAN REGAIN our balance and realize our wholeness when visiting a forest. We can be receptive to feeling connections with all living forms. By watching and listening to the squirrels, frogs, chipmunks, and birds, we can hear the soundless rhythms of every living essence. Together they play a never-ending melody of perfect harmony. It's this harmony that enables us to feel at peace. If we are open, we can feel the pulse of living energies and experience oneness with Nature.

MANY OF US THINK of Nature in terms of surrounding ourselves and our homes with manicured lawns, trees, bird feeders, rocks, gardens, and animals. These are ways we try to touch Nature, because we inherently know contact with Nature is basic for our well-being. We bring numerous plants and animals to live in our homes with us. This helps, but we need to take time to just "be" in Nature.

WHAT I CALL "NATURAL NATURE"—ecosystems that haven't been altered, exploited, or destroyed by humans—exists in very few places on the Earth today.

When I visited Africa, I had the opportunity to experience natural Nature.

I TRAVELED TO AN AREA of jungle in Rwanda, where I allowed myself to intuitively experience natural Nature by connecting with a gorilla.

As the gorilla and I communicated, I knew Nature through his body, senses, and spirit. In knowing the gorilla, I felt the rhythm of the leaves, insects, the soil.

I knew exactly how to move in harmony with other life forms' movements, swaying with the bushes and singing with the trees, moving as an intricate part of the whole. I felt the pulse of bamboo and thick vines. I felt trees' thick greenness oozing into my pores. My gorilla body led me into natural movement—knowing how to be. My pores and the rest of me felt wide open. My spirit experienced and communicated and trusted other beings. I innately knew how to cooperate with life. What joy!

I asked the gorilla to communicate with me about humans and the jungle. He replied, "Humans don't understand how the jungle lives. Energy flows out unto other life forms as theirs flows to me. Humans find this hard to understand. Even when surrounded with trees, and flowers, you find it difficult to truly feel Nature. Being in the jungle's body one can feel its total essence. Many humans feel overwhelmed by the jungle for it has great power and personality. Humans often feel they are being swallowed up here. Yet if in touch with it, you can feel yourself become a part of it. Humans resist and fight the thick foliage, vines, and trees that reach out to harmonize with them. You perceive them as engulfing and become fearful. Everyone in the jungle knows this, senses and feels the humans' fears. In moving with the jungle, you can experience a reawakening of your primordial feelings.

"Humans who come from unnatural environments do not understand what it is they experience when in the jungle. They feel fear, joy, and pain, in a deep way. The pain is about the separation from their family of other species. Their ancestors, of many forms, still live in them in some way. Great learning could transpire between humans and other creatures. It is difficult for you to experience true connectedness with other forms because of the cold, hard, unnatural shapes you live in. It is existing in a vacuum, and if you open there is nothing but more vacuum. Other animals attempt to help, but many humans don't hear. And if they do, they think of it as unnatural and reject their knowingness. They've got it all backwards."

Today, we humans are starting to recall our intimate relationships with other species. Being in Nature and listening to the trees, flowers, and our companion animals is helping to wake us up.

Domestication

HUMANS TEND to domesticate those we can and tame as many other animals as possible. Just as we have separated from Nature, humankind has removed cats, dogs, horses, and others from their niches in Nature.

Cats and dogs keep us company in our homes, and in the midst of car fumes and noise pollution. Bless them.

Animals I communicated with who live in the country are usually more able to romp and run and play in fields and streams—to flow with the Earth's natural rhythm. They have space to be themselves and yet be in a relationship with a human. A Russian wolfhound who resides in the country shared this thought with me: "I love to run free on the land, and that's truly when I am happiest and am who I am."

Here is a sad situation that some animals are put in: Some show horses have never trotted on the Earth's green grass or felt cool streams of water flowing over their hooves. Some exist in artificial environments. One woman I know helps show horses adjust to and enjoy what should be a natural way of living in fields and streams. At first, some of the horses are afraid of these totally unfamiliar sensations. "One horse took hours," she said, "before venturing into water. When the horse finally did, a look of fulfillment and deep sense of peace radiated from her."

Even though many animals have been removed from their natural environments, amazingly, many are still in tune with their bodies and intuitive senses. Yet there are those animals who have challenges due to the environments they live in.

We Are All One

OUR PHYSICAL, EMOTIONAL, AND SPIRITUAL separation from Nature is real in that we have chosen to live outside of Nature; yet it is also superficial, because on a deeper spiritual level all life forms are connected and are one.

We don't have to live in woods or mountains to feel this connection, although spending time in Nature makes it easier because the senses are awakened. Yet we can know what it was—and is—like to experience oneness with Nature because this connection is fundamental and is known in our cells and spirit. We have the innate ability to recall and experience these ancient connections in a conscious way.

There are channels of consciousness that connect all life forms. Consciousness is not limited to the body; it can expand into a forest in Canada though one lives in Texas. Usually we inhibit our natural ability to tap into these channels, yet they are always available.

By accepting and allowing our natural intuitive senses to emerge, we can remember how it was to feel life's rhythm flowing through and around us. Opening in this way lets us truly feel, listen, and sense ourselves and others once again. We can directly experience and nonverbally communicate with other animals in a heart-to-heart relationship.

In workshops I teach on telepathic communication with animals, I verbally guide students into preverbal times. I remain quiet while they directly experience animals and the rhythms of other life forms in Nature. This enables them to connect with their roots and to better understand silent, intuitive communication with animals.

Animals Help Us Remember

ANIMALS ARE WISE TEACHERS who show us the kind of integrated beings we once were. Let us watch and listen to them so we can know the interrelatedness and silent communication that surpasses words. Animals can lead us beyond ourselves and into the flow of oneness, if we will let them. After all, they were here long before humans entered the scene.

Animals are emissaries who remind us about our animal ways. More than any other species, humans benefit from this kind of assistance.

When we realize our connections and natural ability to directly communicate with life forms, how can we *not* change our views or the way we live with other forms of life on Earth and in the Universe? In embracing our oneness with Nature, we truly see that life forms are of equal worth.

THE FOLLOWING POEM came to me while meditating about how to be in harmony with myself and Nature.

Close to Nature As My Own Bone

Everything in this garden is in harmony
plants, stones and deer, even the turbulent
thunder of a river.
Only my waves of discord splash
through their forms, disrupt the air's music
sometimes shake this big sphere.

I bow down to it all, sit in the heart
of soil, embrace a violet or green leaf,
fatten my ribs with something rich and solid.
Silence roots, intertwines
with my wild and wounded soul.
I grab a slice of sun and moon.

Then listen to the wisdom from a snapdragon's
lips, and let the storm sink to the bottom
like a stone tossed into a stream.
It tumbles about in currents until it wears down.
Peace rises to the surface and breaks
open, a lily giving way.

Chapter Three

Attitudes Are Energies

ONE EVENING A FRIEND stopped by to see me and he happened to have a snake with him. The dark, thin, foot-long snake was unsettled and wiggling about in his hands. I asked if I could hold her and he gently placed her in my palms. Immediately, I began to tell her mentally how much I liked and respected snakes, while allowing my inner calmness to flow around and into her slender form. Within a few minutes the snake relaxed and quietly rested across my hands. My friend said he couldn't believe the sudden change in the snake.

Whenever I tell about this experience in my lectures or classes, most people shudder and say, "Oh, how can you touch that slimy thing?" or "Snakes are evil looking," or "I'm scared to death of snakes."

I used to take boa constrictors to events for a zoo. I learned a great deal about people's attitudes. Some comments people made were, "That snake can bite and squeeze you to death," "They swallow men whole," "What an ugly, creepy thing." Boas don't have poisonous bites, nor do they squeeze people to death and swallow people. They coil around small birds, rabbits, or other prey to suffocate and crush them for food.

I was sitting with a boa on my lap at a garden show, and a woman who was walking about twelve feet in front of me suddenly turned toward me and saw *snake.* She let out a bloodcurdling scream. One of the zoo employees went over to comfort and reassure her that the snake wouldn't hurt her. The snake was more taken aback by her reaction and attitudes about snakes than she was by him.

I could physically and emotionally feel the fearful attitudes and feelings people were sending to the different snakes I held. I felt sad. In an effort to protect them, I began enfolding them in peaceful, loving thoughts and feelings about snakes. I told people that snakes weren't slimy and wouldn't attack, but it can be a challenge to move beyond emotionally charged untruths we've been taught about snakes.

At my workshops we talk about myths and how people react emotionally to certain species. By the time people leave the workshop they are able to see snakes in a whole different light. Many will take the step of communicating with them and realize what wonderful beings they are.

Our attitudes come through our voices as well as silent thoughts and feelings about things. Since attitudes are literally a form of living energy, they can have tremendous effects on those around us, as well as ourselves. They are like pebbles dropped into a pond, creating ripples that flow outward and touch everyone.

What do you feel if someone is shooting daggers at you with their eyes—or warm loving rays of light? The point is that you do *feel* their attitudes. This is because our emotional energy rides on our thoughts.

Jennie

Here is an example of how the energy of attitudes affected one dog. Jennie, a bulldog, was feeling self-conscious about her body. I sensed someone was making fun of her. When I asked Jennie's guardian about this, she told me, "The veterinarian makes fun of her whenever I take her in and calls her fat pig. I can never keep her on the table when he wants to examine her." Jennie isn't really overweight.

After receiving this information from Jennie, she decided to change veterinarians. Jennie loves the new veterinarian and now sits quietly on the exam table.

This may sound like a minor thing to us in relationship to an animal, but it was important to Jennie. She was feeling the disrespectful energy of the man's comments.

Overall, animals are much more sensitive to our attitudes than we humans are to each other. Animals feel if someone is sending forth feelings of genuine interest or genuine indifference. Animal companions can be greatly affected by the vocal and mental attitudes we send outward. This is why it's paramount to explore our attitudes.

Our attitudes and responses toward animals are formed in early childhood. Parents, friends, churches, and other institutions influence us. And since attitudes are currents of energy flowing outward, they easily affect us as children. The educational system teaches us how to reason and remember facts, but unfortunately does not support our intuitive gifts. In school we are taught a scientific point of view that teaches us to think of animals as objects or tools to be used by humans.

One reason the human race thinks it's the most superior form of life is language. Many view animals as dumb, undeveloped beings because they lack the ability to speak. But human language may just be a biological or genetic ability that is different from other forms—one that we simply happen to possess. Language isn't unique, superior, or so fundamentally different from a dolphin's sonar, a wolf's howl, a cat's keen eyesight, or a bear's incredible sense of smell.

Fruit Bats

ONE OF THE MOST enriching experiences I've ever had was with two bats. A friend and I were going to transport them from one zoo to another. The moment I saw them, I felt a kinship with them. I was extremely impressed with the man who was caring for these beings. It was obvious he had taken time to develop a friendship with both bats.

It was the first time I had been this close to bats and I was eager to communicate with them. I watched these greatly feared animals hang from his shoulder and ever-so-gently eat fruit from his fingers. I was totally amazed at their fragile, silken wings, their gentle spirits. My friend drove to the other location while I sat in the back of the van admiring these wonderful new friends. Their rich brown eyes touched mine in a way that allowed the three of us to share a flowing communion of love.

Categories, Language, and Biases

IN OUR MINDS and with our words, we tend to separate everything into categories. It's easy to fit our feelings, the world, and other forms of life into our neatly packaged phrases and perceptions. As a result, words distance us from direct experience, and we can end up limiting ourselves and our experiences.

If we think language can only be voiced, written, or communicated by body gestures, it sets up confining boundaries for ourselves. The terms and labels we apply to everything and everyone restrict not only us, but our animal friends as well. This can stop us from seeing animals as they really are and hinder them from fulfilling their potential. Animals may "live down" to their person's beliefs and expectations about them.

We have many groundless biases and prejudices about animals. Some animals we think of as good, and others evil. Some animals are loved while others are hated.

Some are described as beautiful, some as ugly. If we set aside our limiting views, we can see animals from a balanced perspective.

Humans usually exterminate the bad and the ugly and sometimes try to preserve the good. But as we are finding out, some "bad" beings we destroy are turning out to be "good." We are discovering each life form plays an equally important role in an ecosystem to maintain order and balance.

Views about animals vary from culture to culture. Some Chinese serve dogs for dinner while Westerners coddle dogs like children. Westerners eat cows while Indians believe they're sacred beings to be respected. Some Spaniards think of cats the way Americans think about rats, whereas most Westerners enjoy cats' company.

The more human-like an animal is, the more intelligent and alive they seem to us. Again, we assume the human mind and form are superior. In reality, the various forms that life flows through are different yet equal. One terrier had this to say about the human form: "I've been in human form before, and I don't think it's really anything special. In fact, it was constricting in many ways."

We assume if an animal is large that it's somewhat intelligent. When we compare a chimpanzee to a caterpillar, which seems more intelligent and alive? The chimp. But if we look beyond the form, this isn't true. (Here I am referring to Universal intelligence that flows through all life forms, which is different from the intellect as based on and measured by human standards.)

While roaming through the woods one day, I noticed a caterpillar moving up the trunk of a tree. As I communicated with her, I could feel her senses and see through her eyes. Our body moved in a fluid, wave-like motion. We inched up several branches and twigs, feeling along the way for a high, safe place to spin a cocoon. We finally found a twig that was sturdy and safe. Inwardly, it felt like the right place.

This caterpillar found her special spot by moving in harmony with Universal intelligence and rhythm. She "felt" her way to the best place.

We think intelligence and the way we use reason are superior in comparison to other animals. But most of us can't fathom how infinitely intelligent other animals are. Let us think about the many talents and natural abilities they utilize that we don't possess or use. What about the way a monkey moves with agility and grace from tree to tree, or how a bird rides on the wind's currents?

Western society thinks that animals are not very intelligent. Therefore, animals themselves are considered to be of little value.

Humankind's pattern from the past is to use all other forms of life. They are only valuable if they fill some human want or desire. We exploit animals for economic gain. Animals are used for food, sport, fur, research, medicine, and entertainment.

Some dog and cat breeders breed for beauty and financial gain, while an animal's temperament is given low priority. As a result, many breeds today suffer from genetic and biological problems that are passed from generation to generation. This is a clear reflection of our society's values.

We tend to view evolution in a linear way. Evolutionary charts begin with what's considered the lowest form of life and progress through many forms in between, with humans at the very top.

The wheel I described in the last chapter is a more accurate way to view evolution. Every living being is a spoke on the wheel. No life form is higher or lower than another on the ever-turning wheel of life.

In fact, we may think we are the only ones who have evolved. We forget every species is continually evolving—including humans. Let us respect and allow other animals to pursue their evolutionary path as we are.

MANY ARE ATTACHED to our notions of what a dog, cat, hamster, or cow is like and how they should act. For example, when people think of a cow they think of something that manufactures milk and meat. Unfortunately, we get stuck in the form and fail to see the being inside the form.

A woman contacted me to communicate with a cow friend. Sally had watched Josie, the cow, enter this world, and they have experienced close ties for fourteen years. Sally wanted to know more about their relationship, since she was the only human Josie would allow close to her.

Josie is a wise being who was delightful to communicate with. Her thinking is quick and clear. Josie nonverbally told me how important her relationship to Sally is. This is what she said to Sally through me: "You are my primary connection with humans. I can trust you. We opened up to each other and have shared many meaningful experiences together." Josie ended by communicating the following message from her inner wisdom: "Remember that life moves through various forms. Whether life flows through a cow, horse or bird, life is life. The form itself is irrelevant in many ways because it's the spiritual being that's important.

Let us accept and respect all life forms. Look into their souls. There's a deep bond between all life expressions."

Opening to Possibilities

OPENING TO POSSIBILITIES is what allows silent communication to happen. This is why children can easily and naturally communicate with animals. They know they can do it. By tapping into our inner child, we can experience the world of limitless possibilities.

The silent language of intuition, which involves inner senses and vision, is an avenue to know an animal as a member of a species and as an individual.

Since beliefs and feelings are energy, imagine how important it is to understand what our attitudes about life and animals are based on. Then we can honestly question our attitudes, and alter them if we want to.

As new attitudes are nurtured, they can grow, flow, and continue to evolve in their own timing. True attitude shifts are felt from within. Being open and aware can empower change, which invites us to communicate, in a real way, with other life forms. We can recall what we already know is true about animals.

Cues from Attitudes

ANIMAL COMPANIONS TAKE THEIR CUES from our attitudes. What we send out to them, we will see played out in some way. For instance, if I think my animal is bright, dumb, sick, healthy, gentle, or vicious, that is what I encourage and draw out of her. If I think mice are pests, they will play the part of being pests. And as with people, it's difficult for the animals to break out of expectations—whatever they are.

A woman who attended my workshop on telepathic communication with animals said that one of her greatest fears was that her cat, Indigo, would get run over by a car in front of her house. I suggested she get in touch with and understand the basis of her fear in order to discharge the energy being projected onto Indigo. But within a month, Indigo was killed by a car in front of her house. Unfortunately, this woman's intense fears had become forms of energy that manifested her worst expectations.

KATHY TOLD ME she didn't feel her horse, Pinta, was performing her best at shows and wanted to know why. She mentioned that if Pinta didn't improve she might sell her.

When I asked Pinta about her performances, she responded, "I feel wonderful about the shows. My person worries too much about the shows and gets so intense that this affects me. I am willing to do my best, but her wavering energies influence my performance. She doesn't let me know in a clear way what's expected of me. When she lacks confidence, so do I. When she feels I won't perform well, I don't. Since she is thinking about sending me away, I feel confused and in limbo as she does. She's not putting her all into our relationship and I know this."

When I told Kathy what Pinta's responses were, she said Pinta's comments were true. This communication helped her to better understand Pinta's feelings. I told Kathy she needed to decide if she was going to keep Pinta, and if she did, to make a commitment to their relationship. Pinta was willing and waiting.

Kathy decided to keep Pinta. As Kathy began shifting her attitudes, Pinta did too. Her show performances improved within just a month.

Workshop Exercises

IN WORKSHOPS, I guide people into the experience of becoming an animal so they can sense life from an animal's perspective. After this experience, people begin to question their old views. This happens because their experience of becoming an animal doesn't match their attitudes about what animals are supposed to be like. Many times I can actually see their attitudes begin to shift.

I ask people to spontaneously write down beliefs they heard or were taught about animals as children. Some of the attitudes poured out onto paper were: Animals are dirty, uncivilized, lowlife, biters, to be feared, dumb, unfeeling, unthinking, mean, trick performers, smelly, messy, soulless, uncontrollable, distrustful, shedders, and violent. Other attitudes mentioned were: animals are to be kept outside, they are expendable, and they only serve a specific purpose. For example, cats are good to keep around to catch mice.

From these exercises, people realize how affected they are by beliefs that are fed to them when young. Most see how they have viewed, labeled, or treated animal friends as inferior beings. Some feel guilty about this, but I tell them to let it go since they didn't have the awareness until now. From this point, they can let the insights become reality through their thoughts on and actions in relationships with animals. Then I ask the participants to jot down qualities they see their companion animals express.

Here are some qualities they saw in their animal companions: Joy, spontaneity, caring, playful, magical, nurturers, real, protectors, giving, forgiving, and happy.

At some point during my workshop, an animal and I will romp around the yard, while people use their inner senses to feel the qualities that flow naturally from and through the animal. This helps participants to use their inner intuitive sight and senses that open in a new way, which allows them to truly see within that animal's Nature.

I ASKED ZOE, a collie, if he would participate in my workshop on communication with animals. He was pleased and excited about the prospect of helping humans learn.

I asked everyone to stand in a circle and verbally guided everyone into a state of relaxation so they could move into their intuitive senses. Then I asked them to be receptive and to expect to receive communication from Zoe.

Zoe was seated in front of me and I telepathically and verbally asked him to communicate with us. As he remained seated in front of me, he looked from person to person to let us know he heard our request. (There were twenty of us.) Then Zoe stood up, wagging his tail, and walked around the circle, deliberately pausing in front of each person.

Next, Zoe leapt out of the circle, barked, rolled around, and wiggled on green grass. He was a living example of total openness and receptivity to all life. Zoe was showing us how to let down the defenses that most of us begin building when young. He communicated to me how painful and difficult it can be for animals to try to penetrate our barriers before humans can hear them. Unfortunately, we don't often hear them, and if we do it's easy to think it's our imagination. But this is beginning to change as many people are seeking to connect with their animal companions in a nonverbal way.

All of us heard Zoe's silent teachings loud and clear. Everyone was awed by the simultaneous, perfect synchronization of his outward actions with his telepathic messages. Zoe is a great teacher.

If we treat animals as the intelligent beings they are, they will share with us.

When Attitudes Transform

IF WE ALLOW OUR ATTITUDES about animals to transform, a door of limitless possibilities opens and we can genuinely relate with animal friends. Building relationships with other forms of life is the best way to learn about them. In becoming more aware, we can allow animals to express their whole being. Only then can we relate as equal companions, friends, teachers, and students.

Animal ambassadors like Zoe show us how to regain our forgotten spontaneity, playfulness, compassion, enthusiasm, and love. They offer us the opportunity to reconnect with both inner and outer nature.

Intuition reaches depths that go beyond words. It is a universal language of spirit and heart that bypasses mind and ego. Communication with animals is an exchange of spontaneous feelings, pictures, knowingness: a mutual understanding between spiritual beings.

My own companion animals have taught me how to be more spontaneous, open, and receptive. And I feel the unconditional love they express to me. What better gifts or lessons can one receive in life?

We must be willing students before the animals can teach us. Animals have been on Earth much longer than we have and can teach us how to live in harmony. Let an animal companion be your leader and teacher for a day. You will see and experience them and life in a different way.

As one cat put it,"Sometimes I teach you and other times you teach me."

Animals usually live out their part naturally in relationships to people. And there are times when an animal has problems that prevent him from relating well. But often communication breakdowns are due to human attitudes and misperceptions. Everyone is cheated when this happens. By consciously exploring our attitudes, we can choose to create an atmosphere of love, acceptance, and equality. Our inner child, the part of us that is playful and spontaneous, knows how to hear what the animals say and can experience meaningful relationships with them.

Our attitudes are the key, and they can make all the difference in and for the world.

When I was first learning how to communicate with animals, Chloe would lovingly say, "You still have a ways to go, my friend."

Chapter Four

Animal Nature

IN THIS CHAPTER I present material that has come from communicating with animals. We will also look at what the animals have allowed me to experience through their senses.

Our culture attempts to understand animal Nature by having animals perform various experiments that involve learning and problem-solving capabilities, but such experiments do not show us true animal Nature because they are conducted in unnatural settings and situations. Animals are asked to perform behaviors that are not natural in their environment.

The testing instruments used to measure intelligence come from our standards, and the results are based on what we feel intelligence is. For us, the ability to reason is the pinnacle of intelligence. Yet intelligence is the life force that flows through every living being. Intelligence does not depend on the size of a brain, or even if a being has a brain. Being aligned with and living in harmony with all of creation *is* intelligence.

How would we measure up to animals' tests? A lioness might ask us to stalk an antelope, or a monkey might request us to climb and swing through trees in the rain forest, or a cat might tell us to catch mice in a barn. According to such tests, we wouldn't be rated as very intelligent beings.

The behaviorist point of view used to be that a conscious experience couldn't be observed directly; therefore, it couldn't be studied scientifically. When people subjectively thought they were seeing an animal experiencing conscious thoughts or feelings, it was called anthropomorphism. Today, this attitude is shifting, and people studying animals are realizing how intelligent they truly are. Yet many people are still thought to be naive if they believe animals are conscious of themselves and what they do.

T. C. Schneirla, world authority on army ants, says that this particular species of ants domesticates animals as we do cows. They cultivate agricultural crops and carry parasols on hot days. Ants have taught us lessons in architecture, cooperation, and patience. But because they do not look like us, many still assume they are not very intelligent or aware, and do not have the capacity to learn. This way of thinking leads us away from understanding animals in a meaningful way.

Animals still know and understand their relationship to Nature and her inner workings. They can teach us about ourselves and help us to return to our roots in Nature.

Instinct and Awareness

THE TERMS "INSTINCT" or "genetic programming" were and still are sometimes applied to almost every animal's behavior. There are certain instincts that exist within every species, including us; for example, a newborn's desire to suckle and cry, or the instinct to survive. Yet some use this term to explain most animal actions.

Nonhuman animals are not born with instincts only. Inborn concepts and impulses guide each animal's behavior in varying gradations. Many animals must learn some of their behavior and culture from parents. Female apes must learn from their mothers, as we do, how to nurse and care for their infants.

When humans speak of instinct, it often implies that animals are unaware creatures. But instinct is simply a different kind of intelligence. Who can say which qualities and abilities are better than another's? All beings act in ways that are best suited for their body, mind, emotions, spirit, and purpose.

I asked a deer if she was aware. Her response was, "Are you? Sometimes you are, and sometimes you aren't. It is the same with most of us in the animal kingdom. Awareness happens at various levels. If you are walking across the grass, are you consciously thinking about walking, or even where you're going? Yet if an animal does this they are often called unconscious and instinctual. We react to our environment, so do you. Are your reactions instinct? Also, what you call your spirit or soul exists within us as well. You humans try to separate yourselves from the animals, but you are not so different in many ways from us."

Animals know that they are self-conscious beings. Of course, there are varying degrees of consciousness, but one degree is not better than another—merely different. Awareness flourishes within all life forms. Each individual animal is different and, therefore, varies in degrees of intelligence, sensitivity, and other abilities. The same is true with humans.

Both the human and nonhuman animals possess a biological intelligence. Animals are keenly aware of their body intelligence. Humans can communicate with other animals through their sensory intelligence, as well as telepathically. It's a matter of re-awakening these senses.

One horse silently said to me, "Your species limits awareness to the mind, and even that is limited by reasoning. Other animals know awareness in sensory and intuitive ways. All ways are equally important and of equal value."

Animals communicate well through this complex sensory system, while humans focus on using the mind, speaking words. It's easy to get caught in words and logic. The vocalizations and other sensory resonances animals express are not lesser ways of communicating. Animals are aware of directing their voices as we direct words. They are more careful with their voices than we are with words.

Vibrations, Gestures

SOUND VIBRATIONS are something most of us have in common, whether it be a bird singing, a cat crying, or a human humming. Some beings emit vibrations that humans cannot hear with their ears, but can experience on an intuitive level. We are all unique expressions of the life force. Like the instruments in a symphony, our vibrations are expressed in diverse ways that create a beautiful music.

We recognize the importance of human gestures in communication. The animals' gestures are important and a part of their language, too. But it can be easy to misinterpret an animal's gestures. For example, some people assumed my companion cat Chloe didn't like them because she turned away from them and wouldn't sit by their side. She acted this way because she was shy and needed time to know and trust them before sitting by them.

Many minute gestures animals make often go unnoticed by human eyes. Animals' language is richer and much more versatile than our human language.

Spirit, Soul, Group Soul, and Personality

I REFER TO THE DIFFERENT ASPECTS of animals as soul, spirit, and personality. The division is an arbitrary one, for the many aspects of an animal cannot be divided. I have done so for the sake of discussion. We all have various aspects to the Self. When I communicate with an animal, I connect with the whole animal.

Animals are multidimensional souls like us. All souls are sparks of light that make up the whole of the Creator. The Creator continues to experience Itself through all of creation. It is forever expanding and evolving. Each soul is part of a group soul comprised of many souls or sparks that vibrate to a similar frequency, and who are perhaps learning similar lessons. The group works together, in individual bodies, on what one could call assignments. After leaving the body, the spark or essence returns to the group and shares its experience with the group and with the oversoul. We could call the oversoul the leader of the group.

For each species, including humans, there is a collective consciousness level. There is also a consciousness level that all forms of life are a part of, because we're all one in spirit. (When I refer to the term "soul" throughout this book, it is that highest divine energy of who we are that creates our physical forms. When I refer to "spirit," I'm referring to the life force within the body that lifts out after death and rejoins with the soul.)

Our society emphasizes the physical form, but we must remember the importance of the soul. The soul creates the physical form, through which it will experience what it chooses to experience in order to learn. The body eventually dies, but the soul lives on and on.

An animal's soul is not caught in conditioning, personality, or other habits. The spirit and soul of an animal express a clear and flowing wisdom. A cat who had crossed over communicated this message to me for her person: "Even though my body left the Earth plane when it was only three years old, I learned the lesson that love heals all. Thank you for the deep love you showed me. It helped to heal me on many levels."

Each animal's personality involves his or her basic traits, likes and dislikes, and emotions, as well as endearing qualities, quirks, and faults that make us love him or her even more. The personality is concerned about situations and circumstances. Just as no two humans have the same fingerprints, neither do gorillas. Every living being in the Universe is unique.

For example, I communicated with a dog named Harry who told me he loved popcorn. When I questioned Harry's person, she laughed and said that it was true. A cat told me of her love for violin music since she was a kitten, and said it soothed her nerves. Another cat told me she was very fond of a woman named Marilyn. The cat's person was amazed that she mentioned a name, and said Marilyn was a neighbor who often visits them. One dog communicated to me he didn't like the food that his person was feeding him, while another said he wanted to go for more walks.

Specifics like these show us that animals are indeed self-conscious beings, with opinions, likes, and dislikes. I feel a shift in feeling and energy when communicating with these different energetic selves of an animal.

Physical Sensations, Emotions, and Self-Consciousness

MANY ANIMALS HAVE central nervous systems not so different from our own. Animals experience physical pain and other sensations to a greater degree than we do because of their keen sensory systems.

They feel sadness, happiness, grief, and love. They laugh and they cry, they know the pain of loneliness. Animals experience the same spectrum of emotions as humans do.

Some people think animals are only capable of offering superficial love. Yet many animals live and love unconditionally, while we humans often just talk about it. Animals accept us for who we are.

Elephants show great devotion, love, and concern for their families. If a young calf dies, the mother may carry him in her tusks for days, or try to keep lifting the calf up so he will walk again.

When I asked my companion cockatiel Etheria about self-consciousness, she said,"I am more aware than you know. You may not perceive this from me outwardly, but I don't perceive yours outwardly either. Humans get stuck in reactions, the same way you perceive that animals do."

Animals have other interests besides food, water, and survival. They communicate their concerns to me about relationships with their people, other animals, and many other situations that touch their lives. Animals want to enjoy life, play, or perhaps relax/meditate/pray under a tree. Some people chuckle at the thought of an animal relaxing, meditating, or praying, or contemplating a star-filled sky. But if you haven't experienced life from her perspective, how can you know the animal isn't doing what she appears to be doing?

Animals follow their natural tendencies unless they are taught to curb them. It can be difficult for domestic animals to fully flow from their natural tendencies, since they are bred and live in the midst of our cultural conditioning. Since our companions are social beings who live with us, they learn how to control some of these natural tendencies.

Animals develop their intelligence and gain knowledge through experience. We do this too, but since we think of body and mind as separate, we are mostly aware only of what the mind holds, while the animals integrate this as a whole.

Intuition

ANIMALS HAVE THE NATURAL intuitive ability to see into our hearts, and they can know the future. The intuition and extraordinary senses animals possess alert them to any subtle changes in their human's moods or voice. Animals perceive things most people can't begin to imagine. Animals have the ability to look into and to travel in many dimensions and often do. They can see other life forms' energy fields. Animals have the ability to hear thoughts, see pictures, sense intentions and to smell and pick up on emotions. They can see beings living in spirit form and communicate with them on a regular basis.

How does your animal friend always know when it's time to go to the veterinarian's, or if you're going on vacation, or to comfort you when you're sick?

Chloe usually hides under my bed an hour before I have to take her to the veterinarian's.

Dreams and Astral Travel

ANIMALS DREAM about daily routines, other animals, their people, and other things that are relevant and irrelevant to their lives. If I decided to connect telepathically with Chloe while she was asleep, I could see or feel glimpses of her dreams. Sometimes I saw her being chased by or chasing another cat. Animals also are attuned to our dreams. A woman called me because her cat, Snowball, had stopped sleeping with her. She mentioned it was a time of transition and she was having nightmares. When I asked Snowball why she stopped sleeping with her person, she said she could see and feel the nightmares. They scared her.

In the middle of the night, a dog named Clarence literally ran to and awakened his person who was, at that moment, calling him in her dream. This happened more than once.

Animals astral travel while they sleep, and so do we. They travel into other realms for various reasons: to learn, to visit friends who are in spirit form, to heal, to help another, or just for fun. Fish and snails can fly, trees and stones can dance around the moon. The spirit is free to experience what it desires.

Animals who are ill or in pain often leave their bodies at night or even during the day for relief. They run and play, or fly if they cannot do so in their physical bodies. People do the same.

Premonitions

ANIMALS ARE WELL KNOWN for their premonitory powers. They feel when storms or earthquakes are going to occur. Animals' senses keep them attuned to the natural forces. Because of their ability to perceive energy emitted by other life forms, they also sense changes in the Earth's electromagnetic field or within a person's energy field.

David Monagan states in his article "How Animals Predict Earthquakes" that animals have the ability to experience infrasound perception, which are very low sound waves of 100 cycles per second or less produced by foreshocks or the sudden venting of underground gas. He also states that biologist Melvin Kreithen, at Carnegie-Mellon University, and his colleagues discovered homing pigeons can detect and integrate the sounds of thunderstorms and ocean breakers hundreds of miles away into their extraordinary navigational systems. A similar sensitivity has been found in codfish.

Another interesting point Monagan mentions in his article, determined by the late biologist David G. Moulton of the University of Pennsylvania, is that dogs are 100 to 10,000 times more sensitive to certain smells than humans.

Time Perception

ANIMALS EXPERIENCE TIME in a different way than we do. Time is elastic. Many dogs actually live seven years in comparison to what would be one year for us. Flies live for approximately twenty-one days, or longer, if the weather is cool. One of our days might feel like three years or more to them.

Animals and humans can move beyond what we think of as this reality. I have talked with many people who have seen cats, dogs, birds, and other animals dematerialize and materialize. Animals have the ability to move in and out of other dimensions at will. A friend called one day and said, "I was watching my cat sitting in my backyard. She stood up and started walking toward the neighbor's fence. She leapt up and disappeared before her paws ever touched the fence. Then I saw her materialize a second later in the middle of my neighbor's yard."

This is becoming easier for animals and humans to do at will now, because the Earth is laboring through her own rebirthing process. The old energetic shells of density around the Earth are being released. More light is pouring in to help Earth and all life forms to evolve. (More about this in chapter 16.)

Time is an arbitrary system humans set up to give us a sense of order since we live on the physical plane.

Intelligence

Animals are highly flexible and versatile. This calls for conscious thinking and intelligence. Every day animals are faced with unpredictable situations that call for conscious, intelligent assessment, in order to act in the most efficient way for each circumstance. The more experience animals have, the more they will develop those abilities to think and reason through all their senses.

When I'm communicating with animals, they express conscious thoughts and feelings to me. They silently relate their observations concerning circumstances, make judgments about situations, and show other intentional behaviors in relation to their lives. Animals plan ahead and anticipate other life forms' reactions, and also events.

Most animals are conscious of their actions but may not always understand why they did them. Sound familiar?

This example of animal intelligence is taken from the book *Language Barrier: Beasts and Men* by Elizabeth Mann Borgese. Professor Richard Herrnstein of Harvard, in an article ("In Defense of Bird Brains") published by *The Atlantic Monthly*, wrote that pigeons were trained to look at 35 mm color slides and to "report" whether there were any human beings in the picture or not. The slides were from all parts of the world and presented various sorts of settings and backgrounds. The human beings were men, women, and children of all races. Sometimes they were visible in the far distance; sometimes they were almost totally covered up by intervening objects. The precision of these animals was amazing. "More than once we have found," writes Herrnstein,"that we had misclassified a picture ourselves, either by failing to see a hidden person or seeing one where there was none, only to be corrected by our pigeons."

Chimps who learn American Sign Language and try to grasp syntax are like us trying to learn their vocalizations and to structure them in the same way they do. Animal sounds and vocalizations have structure and rhythm, as words do for us. We just don't ordinarily perceive or understand them. The animals do much better at learning and understanding our language than most of us ever do with their languages.

Purpose

EACH ANIMAL IS a spiritual being who has a purpose and mission to accomplish while on this Earth. (Here, I am generalizing to offer some examples, but each animal has a specific mission.)

I have communicated with a number of cats who are like monks. They spend a great deal of time sitting in window sills or in gardens meditating and praying for others, as well as for the world.

A number of dogs I've communicated with tell me they are here to spread love, joy, and healing light to the people and animals they live with in a household as well as in the neighborhood and the world.

Some think of animals as simply lying around or being lazy, but they are often doing their work when they might appear to be dozing or sleeping. Their work often includes working in various dimensions.

Directing Energies

SOME SPECIES OF FISHES, birds, and whales know how to work in a collective, cooperative network, linked through various intuitive biological connections and energies. They retain their individuality, yet have learned to do a dance of harmony with each other, the wind, water, and sky.

Wild animals direct and utilize their life force in fluid, economic, proper ways. There are domestic animals who also direct their energy in clear ways, but many get caught in our cultural thoughts as well as peoples' ego patterns.

Animals are typically straightforward in their telepathic conversations with me. Most do not lie, although some domestic animals have learned from us to play emotional games. Animals have learned how to manipulate us at times in order to get attention. I've watched dogs limp when their people are in the room to gain attention, but as soon as their people leave the dog walks normally. Usually, it doesn't take many questions from me before they explain their actions.

Most animals naturally love and accept themselves.

Animals walk the Earth and live by a code of ethics that is admirable. Animals have the wisdom and innate intelligence to live in harmony with each other and the land. Usually, they take only what they need.

Animals don't create wars and aren't destroying the Earth. Humans have violated every living form, including the Earth herself, which is something nonhuman animals innately know not to do.

Memory

ANIMALS REMEMBER EVERYTHING that has ever happened to them. Some memories remain conscious while others become unconscious. Old memories can be brought into conscious awareness in order to help release the animal from emotional trauma. Memories are also recorded in every cell of the body. When dealing with emotional issues, it's important to help the body release the emotional pain or blocks from an unpleasant memory. This can be done through a number of the techniques described in the "Understanding and Supporting the Animals We Love" and "Soul Recovery" chapters.

If we look beyond an animal's emotional problems, they retain all of their species' memories, knowledge, and innate urges within their spirit and emotions and on a cellular level.

Power of Choice

MANY DON'T THINK of animals as having the ability to make choices, and most of the time we don't allow them the freedom to do so. But animals can and do make choices. When it comes to altering behavior, they can consciously choose to remain in the old behavior or change it with the help of their person. Of course, it can be difficult for an animal to change if their human stays stuck in old patterns. But if the person is willing to look at and adjust their patterns, the animal can change with more ease.

And though there are many similarities among us, let us remember to respect and honor the differences.

Love

I AM ALWAYS MOVED by the essence of each and every animal I communicate with. I continue to learn a great deal from them. Love, joy, friendliness, forgiveness, and spontaneity spring forth from the depths of their hearts and souls. Animals know how to live and enjoy life. Let us watch and learn from them. They can open our hearts and set us free. If we treat our animal friends as the equal spiritual beings that they are, we can discover the depth, the simplicity, and the complexity of their true Nature.

Chapter Five

Mirror, Mirror

JANE CALLED ONE DAY wanting to know if I would have any insight into an "unusual" experience involving her dog, boyfriend, and herself.

"I've been dating Jim for about a year. He and my dog, Mindy, get along great. In fact, she often sits on Jim's lap. The other night when we were at my house, Jim and I had a big disagreement. I was really mad and didn't talk to him for a long time.

"Jim stood up to go get something in the kitchen and Mindy tried to bite him twice."

Jane said she and Jim were concerned because nothing like this had ever happened before.

"Talking about Mindy's strange behavior opened up the door for us to discuss our disagreement in a friendlier way.

"At this point, Mindy suddenly jumped onto Jim's lap, licked his face, and curled into a ball to go to sleep."

Mindy had expressed Jane's bottled-up feelings toward Jim. When I told her this, she laughed and said, "I thought that might be it. Mindy's actions seemed to coincide with whatever I was feeling at the time."

Our attitudes, thoughts, and feelings are alive and filled with energy. Animals are so sensitive and highly attuned to us, they are subject to our influence. This instance shows how animals absorb our attitudes like sponges.

After years of dealing with many people/animal communication misunderstandings, I saw how most animals mirror their person or people. Animals look like, walk like, and speak volumes about their person.

At times, it's difficult to recognize our own reflection.

The first time my cat companion, Chloe, saw her reflection in glass, she hissed and growled at the other kitten in the mirror. It took her twenty minutes to recognize and realize she was feeling threatened by her own image.

We, too, hiss and growl or cry and smile when reacting to our reflections in others.

Sometimes, clients want me to fix their animal's "crazy behavior" without understanding how they influence the animal's actions through their conscious and subconscious attitudes about themselves and life.

Unconscious emotions are potent and their energy empowers and rides with our thoughts. The energy has to go somewhere, and unless appropriately channeled it can directly affect an animal friend.

We do play a role in molding an animal into our own image. Unresolved struggles sometimes are played out through the family kitten, dog, horse, or child. The animal plays it back to us like a movie, with a barking or growling soundtrack.

Animal reflections keep us in touch with our conscious and less conscious self. More often than not, it's the guilts, fears, angers, and the unrealized feelings, sometimes from childhood, that get bound up and hidden from sight.

Unfortunately, many of us are not aware that these deeper feelings can end up being projected onto our animal friends.

For example, three stray cats adopted a couple of friends who live together. Whenever they conceal resentments or other uncomfortable feelings toward each other, the cats bicker and take swipes at each other.

After they "air out" their feelings, the cats return to living in harmony.

One friend called to tell me that her husband was moving out of the house. Within a day of his moving out, their beloved cat, who was closest to him, also moved out for good and was never seen again.

Reflections

Sue and Bruce were experiencing extreme conflict in their marriage. Sue wanted out. She had a very difficult time in directly expressing her anger to Bruce. In fact, she swallowed it most of the time.

One day Sue called me and said, "I'm upset about our lovebirds. They're starting to act crazy, pecking at each other. So much is going on, I'm still trying to get Bruce out of my life once and for all."

I told her the birds were probably picking up all their feelings and needed to be in a quieter place since birds are so susceptible to what's in their environment.

When things seemed to be at their worst for Sue, tragedy struck.

Sue got out of bed early one morning, walked into the living room and could see only one bird in the cage. Sue hurried over to the cage to find the male lovebird's still body lying on the bottom of the cage. The female had attacked and killed him during the night.

Sue could see before her eyes her own reflection of intense anger and desire to get rid of Bruce forever.

Sue asked her veterinarian what happened and his response was, "What's going on in your house? Birds really react to what's around them."

Unfortunately, by the time she realized what had happened, it was much too late for the lovebird.

This unusually dramatic instance shows how unresolved feelings and intentions can be absorbed and acted out by our animal companions.

NANCY CALLED ME to find out what was going on with her dog. Whenever she left town for a few days every month, her dog, Leah, would stay with her mother.

Every time Leah came home she acted tired. She would sit and stand very slowly and move very carefully.

This only happened when Leah had been staying with Nancy's mother. But within two or three days of returning home, Leah would romp, jump, and play again. Nancy had Leah checked out by a veterinarian several times and there were no physical problems.

As you've probably guessed, Leah was remarkably tuned into Nancy's mother who sits, stands, and moves ver-r-y carefully.

JOHN, A SALESMAN, usually takes his beloved boxer Norma with him when calling on clients. When he occasionally leaves her home alone, she dines on the couch and pillows.

As I watched Norma lead John around by her leash, it was crystal clear who was queen of the household: whatever Norma wanted—Norma got.

John worked from his office at home; and so they spent most of their waking hours together. Norma would lie next to his desk and demand to be petted. Sometimes Norma would leap onto his desktop, lie directly in front of him, and stare into his eyes. He would have tremendous trouble getting her down because he "didn't want to hurt her." She sure had him well-trained.

I asked John why he constantly gave in to her demands.

"Well, I really don't. Well, she doesn't like to be alone. Well, why not give in?"

John also played tug-of-arm games with Norma which encouraged her chewing habit. I asked Norma to communicate to me about the chewing and she said "Chewing-the-arm game is a way I can relate to John and I continue it when he's not here. I feel scared and frustrated when I am left alone."

Norma chews on things that contain her guardian's scent. This way she can feel close to him when he's not around. "When I was small I was alone a lot and got shipped off in a crate before I came here. When I got here, someone was always with me, so now it's more difficult for me to be alone. I feel I'm a part of John."

I told John what Norma had shared with me. He said she had been shipped to him in a crate as a young puppy and hadn't had much contact with people. John felt her problem was due to this trauma.

Yes, it started there, but John had recreated much of himself in Norma and she was now an extension of him.

He said, "When I got Norma I felt badly for her because she had been alone so I decided to spend quite a bit of time with her."

Norma's separation anxiety wasn't a form of domination over John, but her power games in his office were.

John adored Norma. And without knowing it, he had fallen under her "dominant spell." This is easy to do when we love our animal companions.

His actions encouraged emotional and physical dependence on him. Because of this, Norma didn't know how to be alone or how to entertain herself. She didn't know who she really was as a dog.

As John started opening up and telling me about his own attitudes and feelings he commented, "It's funny, but I hate being alone. Sometimes I go out and visit clients just to be around people. I also smoke a lot when I'm alone; it makes me feel better. I've tried to quit many times, but just can't do it."

Bingo! John had just unknowingly revealed an important part of what was going on here. Norma was reflecting John's fears back to himself. He was attempting to fill his fear-based needs in order to alleviate his own anxiety about being alone.

John chain-smoked—Norma chewed pillows.

It was a traumatic contrast for Norma to spend a great deal of time with John and then to experience being alone. It intensified her fears and frustrations.

Also in other conversations John kept saying "Norma just doesn't like to be alone."

When I suggested to John that Norma was acting out his struggle of being alone, he couldn't see or accept that his behavior was directly connected to "her problems."

I suggested he stop playing tug-of-arm with Norma because that only inspired her to chew. Also, I suggested ways that would allow her to experience him as alpha figure.

To deal with separation anxiety, I asked John to teach Norma how to be by herself when they were at home. He could do this by putting her in a stay position and walking several feet away from her, then going back and praising her. He could continue to slowly increase the distance until Norma could be in a different room by herself and remain calm. Then he could eventually leave the house in gradual increments of time. Another recommendation was to pretend that he was leaving the house, put on his coat and walk around the door, but then take it off and go back to his daily routine. In this way, Norma could relate differently to what were, for her, anxiety cues.

A few days after John put these suggestions and some other advice into action, Norma totally stopped chewing. They were learning to relate in new ways.

Then I got a call from John. "She's started again." After some discussion, it was clear that John had slowly slipped back into his old ways of relating to Norma. He simply couldn't stand to see her alone in another room, or not to pet her while working. "I'm not giving her all the attention she wants when she wants it," he said, "but maybe a little more now."

John just couldn't release the deeper fears that caused him to be afraid of being alone. His struggles became Norma's struggle.

Since John was not able to face and resolve his fears, neither could Norma.

None of us is perfect and we all do the best that we can. There is no blame or judgment about all this, but only learning and growing in a way that we and our animal companions can actualize our best selves. All forms of life are mirrors for one another so we can know and understand each other.

JOAN SAID, "My male cat is urinating all over my furniture and carpeting. He's ruined about $5,000 worth." She loved Joe and wanted to work things out, but was thinking of getting rid of him. The veterinarian found no physical problem to explain Joe's actions.

She and I talked about problems in her home. Tom, her son, was an incredibly angry twenty-three year old. He was like a volcano always ready to erupt.

Tom and Joe were close friends. Tom would sit and spout off his anger and frustration about his mother, work, and home life to Joe.

I asked Joan to notice Joe's behavior when Tom was feeling angry. Sure enough, when Tom was "pissed off," so was Joe, all over the living room. Joe was making a statement for Tom about his feelings towards his home life and mother.

Joan's angry, resistant attitude toward Joe's and Tom's behavior only made matters worse because it focused on and therefore energized the problems. Tom and Joe knew their actions were getting them lots of attention. Attention is attention—positive or negative.

I suggested to Joan that she begin to relax and feel her intuitive self that knew how to blend with Tom and Joe, rather than encouraging the emotional blocks through resistance. This would discharge some of the energy of the situation.

"I worry every day when I go to work that I'm going to find a mess when I come home," said Joan. This reinforced the urinating since she was visualizing it in her mind. Because Joe saw her mental picture, he gave her exactly what she expected.

I asked Joe to communicate his feelings about the situation. "I cannot stop his anger and confusion that comes into me. I feel overloaded. And the woman is thinking of getting rid of me, like she wants to do with her son. I am reacting to their emotions and marking my territory because I'm afraid she'll get rid of me."

I suggested Tom see a counselor. If Tom could recognize and deal with his emotional patterns, and if Joan could see how she subconsciously encouraged them, both would have a chance to resolve issues and relate in constructive ways. Otherwise, it would remain a stalemate situation. Tom could vent his feelings by exploding, but Joe's only way to release was by urinating.

I suggested Joan visualize Joe using his litter pan and reassure him that he was an important family member.

As Tom showed steady improvement with counseling, so did Joe. After a couple of months, Joe stopped urinating on the living room furnishings.

All three now enjoy a more peaceful life in their home.

Lighten Up

If I have a not-so-hot day, I telepathically and verbally let my animal friends know that my mood isn't related to them or anything they've done. In doing this, I choose to deal with my feelings and not dump my mood onto them.

Many times I snap out of it when they send me pictures, thoughts, or insights that remind me to not be so serious about everything.

One day I was worrying about a difficult predicament. My companion cat, Chloe, jumped up and spread herself out cat-style on the coffee table. I sat down on the couch and asked her if she had any thoughts on my dilemma. She looked deep into my eyes and communicated a clear, loud message, "Look, see how relaxed I am. Stop thinking so much, you're wasting energy. Relax and lighten up." I noticed her take-it-easy position and laughed at myself. It reminded me to let go and flow. It's easy to get entangled in beliefs and emotions.

Jean called me to talk with me about Shadow. She said she often felt scared, sad, and depressed and had been seeing a counselor for years, but depression hung on. She asked me how Shadow, her black feline, felt about living with her. She told me that Shadow was her "significant other."

Shadow communicated directly through me to Jean.

"I wish you would communicate more of your happy feelings to me. I pick up sadnesses from your past and present. It's as though I absorb your hidden 'shadowy' aspects. Let's have some happy times together, because I get bored during the day and want to eat all the time, nothing else to do. I'd like a ball of yarn and a string or two for us to play together. You've forgotten how to play in life. I know you're tired when you come home, but playing would benefit both of us.

"I wish to be a companion but not your all. That does crazy things to me. I feel pressured and overwhelmed, especially when you are overwhelmed. The more dependent you are on me, the more you create my dependence on you. There is a difference between being attached and loving. Practice sending me love and then let go of me.

"I hurt when you hurt and I cry when you cry. And not in such a different way as you might think. Remember, I will comfort you in hard times."

After this communication, Jean took steps to change her life in positive ways. Jean and Shadow play together, which has enhanced their relationship in wonderful ways.

Various Kinds of Reflections

HAVE YOU EVER NOTICED how much animals look and act like their people? When I worked as a licensed veterinary technician, I witnessed this phenomenon time and time again.

One feline female reflected her human female so exactly in eyes, nose, expression, and body that whenever she and her cat entered the hospital, everyone would snicker because it was that obvious.

A strong, virile-looking man made his majestic entrance with his strong, virile-looking Doberman. After an examination, the veterinarian suggested that he have his dog, Brute, neutered for a number of reasons.

The look on this man's face was one of great pain—as if someone had just neutered him on the spot. He said, "No one is going to take away my dog's jewels. I want him to enjoy all the female doggies in the neighborhood. He and I are lady-killers."

Another woman's dog was growling at neighborhood children. I asked the woman how she felt about children and her reply was, "They're a big nuisance."

People may also choose companion animals who reflect physical attributes they would like to possess.

I know a loving, compassionate, six-foot-tall man who owns a tiny two-pound teacup poodle. She sits in his shirt pocket whenever he takes her anywhere.

Steven is a very sensitive artist who weighs about 110 pounds and is approximately five feet six inches. He lives with a huge wonderful husky/shepherd named Big Guy.

One short slender woman, Mary, owns a big Wolfhound mix who weighs more than she does.

Reflections of Physical Issues

OUR INNER TURMOILS can at times be seen in our animal companions' bodies. This is because they may absorb their people's physical ailments.

An extremely sensitive fluffy feline named Molly communicated to me, "I do not always feel well. I am in good health, but sometimes I feel uncomfortable, off and on, when I urinate." She went on to describe the symptoms she was experiencing.

I asked Molly's guardian if she had any urinary problems. She said, "off and on." She, too, went on to describe exactly what Molly had communicated to me.

The way we interact with the animals in our lives is often how we interact with or treat ourselves.

Eileen wanted me to find out why her cat Tanya was obsessed with wanting to eat all the time. The veterinarian reported there were no physical problems.

Eileen felt that Tanya was overweight and wanted to put her on a diet. Eileen said she was overweight and was worried about Tanya's weight. When I saw Tanya, she was average weight.

Tanya communicated, "I feel upset and afraid when there isn't enough food. I get frustrated. I'm so concerned about food. I had experiences in the past where I felt I didn't get enough food. I don't want that to happen again."

I told Eileen what Tanya had expressed. She said "I'm afraid, too, of not having enough food, and I'm thinking about dieting."

So, there was projection here, but also the food issue was a symptom of deeper issues for both of them.

MARY HAD CANCER surgically removed. Some time after discovering the cancer, she found out her dog had the same kind of cancer. He died.

She got another dog. He, too, died of cancer.

Mary said to me, "I'm always worrying about the cancer coming back. I think it's strange that two of my dogs have died from the same kind of cancer that I had. I'm afraid to get another one. Do you think somehow I transmitted it to them?"

Her fear of cancer recurring had manifested through her dogs. It was also possible they had taken on her energies. I suggested she work on resolving her fear of death, which would help her to embrace and focus on life.

Leslie is an extremely sensitive woman who is very connected to her handsome black cat, Ebony. Both experience bouts of colitis. At times, she empathizes with him and takes on his symptoms. When her colon problems begin, so do Ebony's. When Ebony's colitis begins, so does Leslie's.

Leslie said to me, "It's hard to tell whether the colitis is mine or his at times. But I know that I pick up his pain. I try and break the stress-related energy connections between Ebony and me so we don't go in a vicious circle."

The colitis originated in Leslie. However you look at their connection, they are very powerful reflections for each other.

I've dealt with many people whose animals have a similar or exactly the same physical problems as they do. Everything from diabetes, arthritis, and heart problems to asthma and allergies.

When an animal manifests our energy in this dramatic way, it is difficult to ignore.

Shifting Mirror Images

SUSAN LIVES WITH a six-year-old calico, Joy. She called to see if I could help Joy adjust to a kitten she had just brought home. Joy had never really accepted or been close to other animals and few humans. She usually ran and hid.

Joy communicated to me saying, "I don't like the kitten. It's hard for me to be flexible. I never feel settled, safe, or secure. I like to hide in the barn where no one is around. Just don't want him in my territory. I react strongly but don't feel strong. I am scared and must defend myself."

I telepathically let Joy know that she had alternatives and did not have to act in this way. I showed her a picture from my mind and let her feel through my body energy how she could open up and flow.

As I told Susan what Joy showed me through images and thoughts, she smiled and said "It sounds familiar. What can I do to help all three of us to adjust?"

Susan was aware that Joy was acting out her generally rigid ways of relating to people and the world. I said to Susan, "Relax and and let yourself open up and flow. Be patient and loving with yourself and Joy. Rather than resisting her feelings and actions, blend with them. Let Joy be. Yet show her, with gentleness, openness, and mental images that she has choices in acting and reacting. She doesn't have to react from old behavior patterns she feels stuck in."

Susan knew she could help Joy break the mirror imaging by dealing with her own rigid patterns. And she did.

Within a few weeks Joy and the kitten were sleeping together on Susan's bed. The dynamic duo were playing and snuggling. It was a total change in behavior for Joy.

Joy and Susan are transforming and continue to blossom like beautiful flowers. The key is that Susan opened up, which allowed her to understand and begin transforming her patterns. This enabled Joy to feel more open to the kitten, Susan and herself. It's exciting to see all three growing and learning in their relationships.

Being Released from Projections

WHENEVER I SAW my cat companion, Chloe, express some struggling aspect of myself I hadn't learned about yet or seen before, I telepathically said, "I see myself again in you. And I'm sorry if I affected you. I release you from my projections. I accept my feelings, and I'm going to look deep within myself and process this."

Animal companions that live with humans cannot readily free themselves from projections. If we become aware of what we project, this helps to release them. We can understand and redirect projections that release the animals and ourselves to experience healing.

One way to help release animals from thoughts and feelings is to picture in your mind that what you are projecting is a thread connecting you and your animal. Imagine and feel the thread break and dissolve. Believe your animal is freed from the energy. Understand what this reflects to you, then let it go.

What Animals Reflect to Us

Animal companions also reflect our spontaneous, joyful, loving selves. Animals teach and show us about forgiveness and unconditional love. If we allow ourselves to be vulnerable to them, animals can help us feel these life-giving qualities. If we're in touch with our spirit, we, too, reflect vitalizing qualities to animals. It is a circular dance of life.

It's easy to get caught in busy daily routines. We forget to express and exercise our various aspects of being. We need to play, laugh, and have fun.

When we are out of touch with these natural needs, we forget to experience the wonder, the flow, the life-giving energies in ourselves.

MARSHA IS A HIGH-STRUNG woman who resides with a high-strung Doberman, Sam. She called to ask me if there was a way to calm Sam down. I recommended that she take a meditation class. After two classes she called and said, "You won't believe this. I'm feeling much more relaxed, but the incredible news is that Sam is too. When I sit down, close my eyes, take a deep breath and let go of tension, Sam lies beside me and relaxes. I've never seen him so relaxed. I never realized how much I influenced him. I'm glad this is a positive influence for both of us."

The more aware we become of ourselves, the more able we are to listen to and learn from animals. We all learn from each other.

Questions We Can Ask Ourselves

1. DO MY ANIMAL'S physical, emotional state, and/or actions reflect something back to me about myself? Chances are you'll discover some kind of connection. (Remember, if a stray animal has found you, they certainly come to you with their own baggage. But the longer you're together, the greater the chance that a connection with reveal itself.)

2. How am I affecting my friend through my thoughts, feelings and actions? How are they affecting me?

In taking a closer look at living reflections that directly stare at us, we get a clearer picture of what we generate and perpetuate—both positive and negative.

Logic and reason cannot take us into the depths of our feelings, and that is where we need to explore in order to better release ourselves and animals from projections.

3. How do you sit, stand, and walk? How does your body react to various people or situations? Or to the world in general?

The key is to listen to, see, and accept all the different aspects of the self. Experience what the body feels because it's a reflection of inner attitudes.

By allowing deeper feelings to emerge, you become conscious in a new way and more aware of what you're doing with your thoughts and feelings.

If we listen to and befriend our feelings, and direct them in the ways we desire, we awaken and create a solid foundation from which we can become attuned to ourselves and those animals we cherish. This benefits and enhances the overall relationship with respect, love, and harmony.

JOSH IS AN INCREDIBLY HAPPY golden retriever. I fell in love with him the first time I looked into his mysterious, chocolate-brown eyes.

His caretaker, Delores, is a lovely, fluid woman who takes time to stay in touch with her inner thoughts and feelings, and also Josh's.

Delores attended my "Telepathic Communication with Animals" workshop. She said, "It helped me to take a better look at some false attitudes I still have about animals. I don't want them to affect Josh. I want to understand Josh and not limit him through my own projections."

After spending time with Delores and Josh together and separately as friends, I knew that their relationship was built on trust, love, and respect. Their connection deepened as Delores understood more about herself and Josh.

Josh and Delores communicate well because they understand each other through body language and intuition. They have a special commitment to each other, and a close spiritual bond.

Delores befriends her feelings rather than resisting them. She listens and allows her emotions and attitudes to flow through her while remaining centered. She discovers more about her wholeness, which allows Josh to experience more of his wholeness.

Josh genuinely and energetically expresses great joy in being alive, and so does Delores.

This creative inner journey of interspecies communication leads to profound openings, as is the case with Delores and Josh. Let us respect and embrace ourselves and our animal friends with wondrous exploration, love and joy.

We can know a clear and silent understanding that reaches beyond all mirror reflections. Soul to soul. We are all one.

Your animal friend is waiting.

Chapter Six

Telepathic Communication with Animals

GARY AND HIS FATHER were watching a favorite program on TV. Four-year-old Gary stood up and shouted, "I'm coming," and ran to open the basement door.

Tiger, his cat, leaped from the top step into the living room. Gary had heard Tiger's silent request.

Gary's father, a researcher, was amazed at what he witnessed and swore Tiger had not muttered a meow.

As children learn to speak, read, and write, they shift from nonverbal communication into the highly structured world of verbiage and conformity. Children go to school and learn information that they are required to spit out on command. Of course, learning is important, but we're not taught how to listen to and experience all our natural senses. Animals are better at living this way.

Children are usually trained not to trust intuitive abilities, but only tangible proof and facts. Natural intuitive experiences are considered imaginary and end up being squelched. But intuition springs from the imagination. In fact, all our ideas begin in the imagination before becoming a physical reality. Imagination and intuition are what allows interspecies communication to be a reality.

A zebra, one of the first animals with whom I telepathically communicated, said, "Teach the children about animals. They are open to our thoughts and feelings while most adults are not. Parents misunderstand children's words yet their children's perspectives are right. Children understand us."

Communication with animals is a natural way of being, yet it may feel unfamiliar to us. This way seems unnatural and unreal because of false notions we've unquestioningly accepted about our own capabilities and those of animals.

Limiting views block and hinder intimate communication experiences with animals. People can get bogged down in what they were taught a cat, dog, or any other animal should be. They may have trouble seeing beyond the physical form to communicate with the animal. The animals cope the best they can with our limited ways and limited thinking. Let us expand and look beyond the body to see within an animal.

When I was first learning to communicate with animals, I asked for advice from someone who knew all about it.

A wise gorilla spoke to me: "See beyond my gorilla layers to communicate with who I truly am." This enabled me to connect with his essence rather than getting lost in how I expected a gorilla to be and act. He helped me to experience his heartbeat, and his feelings, and thoughts about his life and world.

TELEPATHIC COMMUNICATION is a natural way of communicating. We just need to reawaken our innate inner senses. Other animals telepathically communicate easily with one another. We must remember that we too are animals.

People often sense each others' thoughts and feelings; they're just not aware of sending or receiving them. By consciously using these inherent abilities, it's easy to converse with animals.

Telepathic communication with animals is a language of the heart, to be experienced, not analyzed.

This communication is like a telephone conversation between two people. The telephone wires are the available lines of consciousness open between us that make the call possible. The electrical current, or the energy that the two beings send toward each other, flows through the telephone wires and enables the beings to connect and have a conversation.

Being human, we receive images, words, thoughts, and feelings. Animals can perceive whatever feelings and images we send, since this is the primary perception between us. The vibration, the intention behind the word, is translated in ways that both the animal and we will comprehend.

Guidelines

HERE ARE SOME GUIDELINES to communicating telepathically:

1. Sit in a quiet place with an animal.
2. Center and breathe, being present in mind and body.

3. Create a heart-to-heart connection.
4. Formulate a question.
5. Send the question.
6. Be open and listen, and trust what you receive.
7. Thank the animal.
8. Release each other with love.

Step 1. Find a quiet, peaceful place where there are no distractions for you and your animal friend. Give yourselves time to relax and feel comfortable.

Before communicating, set aside any limiting beliefs you hold about yourself or animals. You might imagine putting those beliefs temporarily into an empty can on a shelf outside of the room, or picture the attitudes dissolving into light. This enables intuition and feelings to flow freely. Trust yourself. Believe and expect that you will have a conversation with your animal companion.

It is also helpful to affirm your intuitive abilities. Sit down, take a deep breath and close your eyes. Next, say and feel this affirmation wholeheartedly seven times: "I have the intuitive ability to create a loving bond with animals and can communicate with them." This awakens intuition, which allows you to open up and feel your inner abilities.

Make sure, intuitively, that you have the animal's attention, and that this is a good time for them. Remember, the calmer you are, the calmer your animal friend will be. An animal whose mind is wandering can't concentrate on what you're saying.

Before communicating, you may want to make eye contact for a few moments with the animal, or touch him or her. Most animals directly sense your desire for communication and are cooperative. Animals may look around the room while communication is going on, but they're usually participating in the conversation. Some animals gaze into my eyes or sit beside me while we communicate.

Step 2. Take a deep breath and center, which is to relax and be at peace. Focus on your breathing. This will shift your attention away from intrusive thoughts and move it toward relaxation of mind and body. This creates open and clear channels for communication to occur. Feel your childlike qualities of being open and spontaneous. Become the playful child who knows anything is possible.

Be totally present, in the moment, in body, mind, and spirit. If you are upset about anything, it's not a good time to communicate with an animal companion. The communication channel could get muddied, and your animal friend might absorb your feelings.

Let's say Etheria, my cockatiel companion, is perched on the chair next to me chirping loudly while I'm on an important phone call. I'm getting annoyed. I take a deep breath and let go of the anxiety to calm my mind, body, and emotions. Then I say, "Please quiet down or fly to another room until I'm off the phone." The key for me is to feel relaxed so I can send a calm, clear message to Etheria. If I were to become more upset and try to quiet her while in this state, she would screech louder.

When people are first learning telepathic communication in my workshop, I ask them to close their eyes. This helps them concentrate and eliminate outer distractions. In the beginning, the animal's presence can itself be a distraction. But with practice, people communicate easily with their eyes open or closed.

Step 3. Create a strong heart-to-heart connection. Look beyond the physical form and connect with the animal's essence. Feel and send love from your heart to the animal's heart. A loving bond is a very real living current that allows thoughts and feelings to flow like water.

While sharing in the heart-to-heart connection, remain centered and grounded. This enables you to remain clear while you send and receive messages, and helps you to not get lost in emotions that can muddy the channel and may confuse or overwhelm the animal.

Step 4. Have a thought or question clear in your mind before you telepathically and/or verbally speak to the animal. The telepathic image, thought, and feeling you're going to send should be crisp and clear. If you decide to also speak the question or message, you want your words to match the image you're sending at that very moment.

Step 5. Send the thought, picture, and feeling simultaneously to the animal. You may want to visualize your message traveling along the heart-to-heart connection as if it's traveling through a telephone wire or on a ray of light. Then let the message go! This way, the animal receives the whole communication with clarity.

If you hang onto the image or feeling, the animal may not get the entire picture and feel confused.

Great! You've just sent your first message, and I bet you're wondering if your animal got it. Since animals are so attuned and receptive to us, they usually receive our message. Remember, whatever you send, clear or muddled, they get.

When I was first learning about communication, I'd send my cat companion Chloe a picture or thought more than once, because I wasn't sure she heard me. She responded by saying, "I heard you the first time." So, trust that your messages have arrived.

We humans experience pictures and thoughts simultaneously, so sending an image and thought to an animal is easy if you relax, center, and direct your image and thought towards the animal. Have fun and let it flow.

See **Exercise I** to enhance your sending abilities.

Step 6. Now you are ready to receive a response. Remain quiet in mind, body, and spirit. Be open and receptive. Imagine yourself as empty, waiting to receive. Allow the heart-to-heart connection and channel to be open and flowing. Listen with your heart, and trust what you receive. Expect to hear from your animal friend. If you don't expect to receive anything, you probably won't.

People find it more difficult to receive than to send messages, because their minds are busy. If you are thinking while trying to receive, you won't be able to hear or see what the animal sends. The animal's messages run into a busy signal, resulting in static. The key is to relax.

See **Exercise II** to enhance your receptive abilities.

Step 7. I always thank animals for communicating with me, because I want them to know that I deeply appreciate what they have shared. This also lets the animal know I received the message.

After we finish our conversation, I imagine the telephone wire of energy dissolving between us, or imagine the animal and me hanging up the phone.

Step 8. After the communication I like to say, "Let us release each other with love." This allows you and your animal friend to move back into your own energy field or personal boundaries, yet remain connected in love.

Exercise I

This exercise will help you develop your sending abilities.

Stand about six feet from a wall and point the fingers of one hand, thumb facing ceiling. Relax the arm, allowing the elbow to bend slightly. Now, feel an irresistible desire to touch the wall, but don't actually move toward it. While feeling this deep desire or intention to touch the wall, imagine your fingertips touching and feeling the wall. You'll sense it when you connect with the wall. Then let go of the connection and come back to your center. This teaches you how to send a thought or image outward. Remember, thought is energy.

Sending a picture, thought, or feeling to an animal is the same as telepathically extending your fingers, touching the wall, and then releasing.

Create an image in your mind and practice sending it outward from your heart to a specific place. When it gets to its destination, let go of it.

By creating a picture in your mind and holding it for a few seconds before sending it, you can build your abilities to concentrate and produce clear visual images.

For people who are not visually oriented, send your message or question and you'll be able to feel when it reaches the animal, like the hand's intention to touch the wall.

There is no right or wrong way to do this. And with practice, you'll find your own way of communicating.

Exercise II

This exercise will enhance your receptivity.

Close your eyes, take a deep breath, and feel your feet firmly planted in the Earth like roots. Then imagine busy thoughts or worries flowing down through your body, like liquid. See them flowing out the bottoms of your feet and into the ground. When you have done this, visualize yourself as an empty glass ready to be filled. Or imagine yourself as a blank tape ready to be recorded on.

You will receive an animal's messages through spontaneous feelings, words, pictures, and thoughts. For example, you may feel what the animal feels (as we sometimes experience with human friends), or hear words and thoughts, or see images pop up like slides on a screen. You may receive messages in all these ways. This is because the senses and the spirit are the means by which we humans can understand nonverbal communication. The key is to be open, to flow and to experience. Listen with an open heart.

When receiving, welcome whatever you get. Don't think, interpret, control, or judge while receiving, since the animal knows if you're accepting the messages. Trust what you get. This encourages the animal to communicate. If you repeatedly question what you receive, an animal could get discouraged and stop sending for a while. How would you feel if someone doubted everything you said to them?

When people in my workshop talk about their communication experiences, some start by saying, "I think I imagined it, but I thought I heard my animal say…"

Most who think they're just imagining have, in fact, connected with the animal. We're just unaccustomed to relating in this wonderfully creative way. Inner trust and clarity come with time and practice.

When people have trouble receiving, some possible reasons are:

- limiting attitudes and expectations about animals
- doubting or trying to control the experience
- expecting not to experience anything
- fear of hearing something hurtful
- being blocked by busy thoughts
- trying too hard

If receiving seems difficult, imagine you and your animal friend carrying on conversations. Relax and let go of doubting or self-critical thoughts that only create blocks. See and feel them flow down and out through your feet and into the ground. Simply allow yourself to open and to experience. Have fun.

Every chance you get, practice sending and receiving pictures, thoughts and feelings.

A short time after I started telepathically communicating with animals, I found myself receiving flashes of pictures, words, and feelings before I had finished sending the thought or asking a question. This comes with practice.

Everyone can communicate telepathically with animals.

Long Distance

In communicating telepathically with an animal, there are no real barriers of time, space, or distance. The only limitations are those that exist in our minds. I communicate nonverbally with animals all over the world whom I never see physically. The connection is established the same way as if the animal were present. It's like a telephone conversation, only it's a long distance call. The animal's name is the same as a telephone number.

This is also true when communicating with an animal who has crossed over into the light. The main connection is always with the animal's spirit. The body was a physical form so the soul could experience what it needed to experience on the physical plane.

Photograph

PEOPLE ATTENDING MY WORKSHOP are asked to bring a snapshot of an animal friend. They look at the picture, close their eyes and imagine the animal sitting in front of them. We could consider this a long distance call. They practice sending and receiving information with the animal. This helps them sharpen imaging skills and know that distance does not limit communications.

Desired Behavior

ANIMALS SEE THE PICTURES in our minds. When working with behavior issues, I will send the animal a picture of the behavior that their person desires—within reason, of course. For example, if a cat is urinating on the carpet for emotional reasons, I will send her images of using the litter pan.

If more than one person in a household is sending a picture to an animal, it's important that they send the same images.

Sometimes, it works better if just one person sends the desired behavior pictures. I've had a number of animals tell me they got confused because their people were sending different thoughts and pictures about behavior.

An Animal's Response

EACH ANIMAL RESPONDS differently to telepathic thoughts and images. Before communicating with an animal, I intuitively sense what the animal is feeling at that time and how she feels about my presence. The majority of animals are open and ready to communicate. Some have a lot of say, while others have little.

The first time I reached out and was able to communicate with Chloe I heard, "It's about time. I've been waiting a long time for you to hear me. Now we can finally talk."

Not many animals have ever been heard telepathically by their people. Animals may pour out feelings and images like a flowing stream when they realize someone's really listening. There are those who need a little time to accept and trust that a human is truly listening. Some animals give up trying to communicate with humans after a while, but will communicate if they are heard.

Other animals may be shy, frightened, aloof, or defensive when they know a person is sending them messages. I've seen outward reactions to this, and can sense it within them.

Animals who initially respond this way have said to me, "You surprised me! I'm not ready to face what you want me to talk about," or "I'm not sure I want you to tell my people what I have to say." A common first reaction is,"Most humans don't do what you're doing."

When I get an apprehensive reaction from an animal, I do not continue connecting with them. I remain within my own energy boundaries and wait for the animal to adjust to my presence. As the animal relaxes, I ask if she will help me and her people understand her feelings and actions.

Take all the time necessary to respect the animal's timing before telepathically approaching them. Rushing into an animal's inner space is inappropriate.

One such apprehensive animal was a cotton-white and gray cat Samantha. My experience with her shows how essential timing and sensitivity are in communicating with an animal.

I stepped into Samantha's house and casually glanced in her direction. Immediately I realized she was an extremely sensitive cat. She was easily affected, like a pool of water. Samantha can be very calm or tossed about like a wave, depending on the state of whoever is around her at the time.

She was overwhelmed by my presence. She knew I could see her thoughts and was scared, so she jetted off to the safe bedroom.

I sat down and talked with her people. Suddenly I heard, "I'm afraid and shy. Not sure I want to talk to you. I'm afraid of many things." Samantha initiated communication with me because she soon sensed I wasn't going to push her. Eventually she roamed back into the room where we were talking. Samantha began to telepathically show me difficult times from a previous home.

We had a friendly conversation. Samantha sincerely wanted to let her people know what was on her mind in spite of her shy and sensitive disposition.

Cutting In

A situation that often arises while I'm in the midst of communicating with one animal is that another animal in the household announces their presence by cutting in. I ask them to please wait until I've finished with their housemate, and then I communicate with them. Sometimes they simply want to chat. Often they will have something important to express to their person.

Keeping Channels Open

We can remain open and receptive to animal friends most of the time because the channel of communication is always available.

One morning I was combing my hair and very involved in thinking about my upcoming busy day. Suddenly, like a mental news flash, I saw the crystal-clear image of cottage cheese on a plate.

A few days before, I had given Chloe cottage cheese on the same plate I was now seeing in my mind. I quickly glanced into the hallway to see Chloe gazing at me. She stood up, meowing, and led me downstairs toward the kitchen. She knew I saw what she wanted for breakfast. I thanked Chloe for getting my attention and said, "I get wrapped up in so many unimportant thoughts. I'm sorry. I want to be more aware of listening to you in our relationship."

I asked Chloe what she thought about the way I listened to her. She patiently said, "Sometimes I interrupt and break into your thoughts so you'll hear me. Once I remind you, you open and listen. You shut me out when you get trapped in constant thinking about many things."

Remember, animals don't send images or thoughts only when we sit down and ask them to. Like humans, animals originate thoughts, images, and feelings when they want to communicate with us.

If an animal companion has something on his mind, is lonely or wants to play, be open to listening. This allows the lines for two-way communication to remain open.

By doing this, both person and animal experience a relationship that's based on a more equal exchange.

Request for Assistance

LEADERS OF MANY and varied species often come to me to ask for prayer. I feel honored when they show up. Sometimes I think this happens because I started the Divine Prayer Line for Animals a number of years ago.

Some nights, as I'm relaxing and drifting into sleep, a representative of a species will show up in spirit form and ask me and others to pray for their species. For example, I've had lions, praying mantises, elephants, tortoises, as well as others appear to ask for prayer. Prayer is a powerful positive energy that is heard and can make a difference in the lives of humans as well as animals.

Asking for a Physical Response

ONE WARM SUMMER EVENING I was at a zoo watching zebras. My first communication experience with an animal had been with a gorilla a week earlier. This was my second attempt, and I wanted to see what would happen.

A zebra was standing quite a distance from me, across the exhibit. I took a deep breath, closed my eyes, and sent her a "hello." Then I asked, "Please walk over to me if you hear me." The zebra started slowly walking straight toward me. When she arrived directly in front of me, she stared into my eyes for several minutes. I was amazed. I thanked her for her willingness to let me know she heard my hello. Later on, I felt embarrassed about asking her to fulfill such a silly request so I could believe, but she was willing. After that dramatic exchange, I trusted my ability to communicate telepathically with animals.

People often ask if animals will physically respond to telepathic requests such as sit, come, or stay. My experience is that it depends on species, breed, personality, situation, and clarity of the image and thought that are sent. Some animals respond often, other animals some of the time, and there are those who seldom respond.

When first exploring telepathic communication with animals, I wanted to find out if they would physically do what I asked, so I recruited my cockatiel friend, Etheria. She said, "That's fine with me." Etheria and I began our trials in a quiet room with no distractions. I would send a clear, sharp image to Etheria of her stepping out of her cage, walking to her left half-way around the cage, stopping, and taking the same route back into the cage. She was cooperative and happy to fulfill the exact image I had shown her.

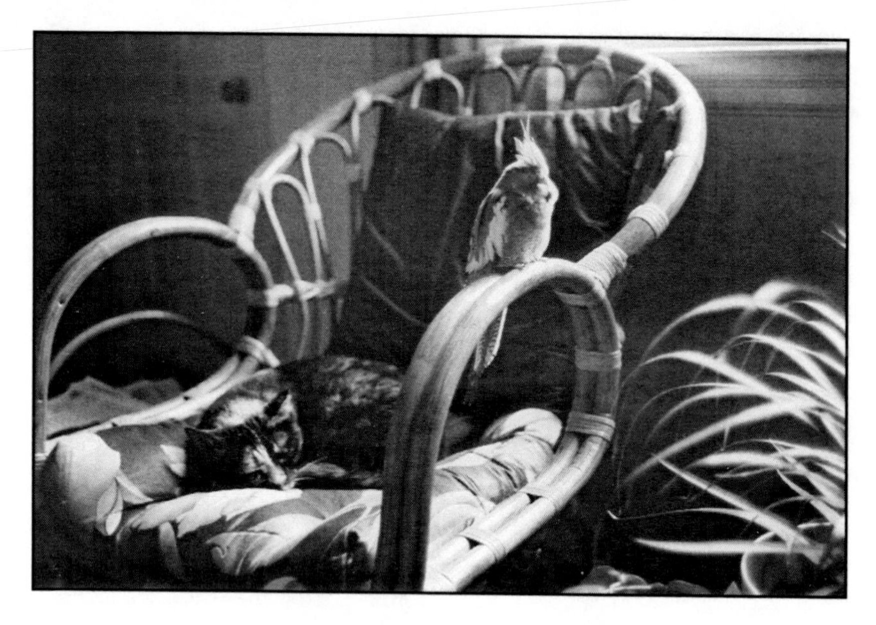

Chloe and Etheria sleeping together.

At times, when I watched TV or was upstairs writing, I'd ask Etheria if she wanted to join me. If she did, she flew to wherever I was in the house. If not, she stayed in her cage. When Etheria knew I was very busy she usually stayed around her cage. Other times, she flew to me anyway, if she wanted some company.

Birds are very sensitive to images sent to them and react to whatever feelings are in their environment.

INTERACTION WITH CHLOE was a different kind of experience, since she was another species and personality. I explained to Chloe that I wished to learn about how she felt when asked to do bodily movements. She said she was willing to take part. Many times she didn't answer my images through physical movement. She'd say, "I don't feel like doing that right now," or "I'm going to sleep." Other times, Chloe would instantly respond to the image and thought I was sending her.

For example, when I wrote this section of the chapter, Chloe was sitting on my desktop. I just flashed an image to her asking, "Wouldn't you be more comfortable lying on your side?" Before I could blink my eyes, she slid onto her side. I guess she thought it was a good idea.

Generally speaking, cats don't care about pleasing their people as dogs do.

ANIMALS WON'T RESPOND physically if the picture sent isn't clear, the person doubts it can happen, the animal has a physical problem, or the animal simply doesn't wish to.

Animals, like people, have varying degrees of will, determination, and cooperation which must be taken into consideration. Some animals have said to me, "I don't want to do what they ask. My person thinks I'm dumb so I'll pretend that I don't understand them."

Asking an animal to respond physically is best done from a willingness to learn from and understand each other, to better communicate with one another, but not for control. Physical actions can be requested for sensible reasons. An outward response from an animal can be valuable for many reasons. One day it could save the animal's life or a person's life.

COMMUNICATION CAN HELP different species to get along physically. For example, when Etheria came into my household, Chloe would take gentle swipes at her. We had a chat. I communicated to Chloe that she needed to respect Etheria as an equal, and to never harm her. And I asked Etheria not to taunt Chloe. Not long after this communication, Etheria began preening Chloe's whiskers and they started to sleep side by side.

Negotiate

YOU CAN COMMUNICATE with ants, mice, cockroaches, and other beings. You can ask them to leave the premises if you don't want them there. But it's important to do this from a place of love and respect, or at least from a neutral place. If this is done with an angry communication, it doesn't work because the beings pick up the hostile energy.

I communicated with ants that were having a good time being in my kitchen. My biggest problem wasn't that they were there, but that I would unknowingly step on them. I negotiated with the leader of the group. (Species have leaders and are the ones to talk to about boundaries and/or situations. The leader receives input from the group or community, and then tells me what's acceptable or not. You can negotiate and find out what will be beneficial for everyone concerned.) The ants agreed to move outside under a pine tree where I placed containers of sweet goodies for them.

You can communicate and negotiate with rabbits who are eating up your vegetable garden, or with moles who are tunneling through your yard. It's important to negotiate in a way where everyone agrees to the terms, if possible.

There are times when roaches or moles might not be willing to cooperate because they don't have anywhere else to go, or don't want to leave the treasures they've found. You need to have a specific place to show them telepathically where they can go, or to have something else to offer them.

One woman called me to say an inspector had found termites in her house. She wanted to know if I could ask them to leave. I communicated with the leader and asked if his community would move into the backyard where the woman would put plenty of luscious logs and other tasty treats for them. (I give ants, roaches, and other beings like this a week to talk it over with their community and then to give me an answer.)

The termites agreed to move. The inspector came back and found no evidence they had been there.

One night, I saw a roach in my kitchen. I told him how much I respected him and his ability to survive in this world. Several nights later I saw a few more of them and laughed. I communicated, "You are really beautiful beings. I won't harm you." A few nights after this, well, there were a few more. I realized what was happening. The roaches were calling to their buddies to come bask in the light of my love and perhaps whatever else might be found: a few crumbs on the kitchen floor. I told them that they were wonderful, but that I would appreciate it if they would return to where they had come from or find an even better place to live. After this communication, they left the premises. Only now and then do I have a visitor.

I learned that my love had attracted them and how to set boundaries that worked for the roaches and for me.

Personality and Soul

WHEN I COMMUNICATE with animals, I communicate with both the personality and soul essence. Sometimes the personality's desires can differ from the soul's desires. Or these aspects of Self may be flowing in a harmonious way.

Some animals will communicate from these different aspects of the Self without being asked. It depends on what the animal wishes to convey to me and her people.

The personality is concerned with things such as food, walks, toys, home environment, and how they are feeling emotionally and physically—all of the things that we are concerned with in order to survive and live our lives.

The soul level is interested in what it is learning or not learning through the physical form. It is interested in fulfilling its purpose for being here.

Candy, a calico cat, communicated that she didn't like the new brand of food that her person was feeding her. She wanted the litter pan to be kept cleaner and asked that the house be kept in better order. Then I listened to her soul, which communicated that it was trying to learn how to be more flexible. Also, that part of its mission was to spread love and joy. Then, there were past-life issues being worked on between Candy and her human family about listening to each other. These two different levels of communication are not at odds, yet there are lessons that the spirit within the body is trying to learn.

Blackie, a twelve-year-old cocker spaniel, whose kidneys were beginning to fail, said he wanted to stay here to continue to help his person, and that he didn't want to leave his body. But his soul communicated this to me: "It's almost time to return home. The body is worn out and my mission is almost completed. The souls in this household will remember the lessons we have all learned this lifetime. I will be removing the spirit from the body soon."

Learning About a Species

IT IS POSSIBLE TO LEARN about any species by connecting with a member of that species. All beings have an individual consciousness as well as the collective group consciousness and vibration that it belongs to.

If you want to learn more about whales, mice, butterflies, or cats, simply communicate with a member of that species and ask them to teach you. You can do the same with plants, trees, and all other life forms. It's really a lot of fun!

Communication

TELEPATHIC COMMUNICATION bridges many gaps, crossing species, cultural, language, and physical barriers. This natural communion enables us to understand more fully what an animal thinks and feels about a person or situation. It can clear up misunderstandings, which often stem from us humans rather than from the animal. Working together in love, all of us can agree on harmonious resolutions. Nonverbal communication adds a dimension to relationships that creates a fuller and deeper connection. Telepathically and heart to heart, we can all experience inter-species connections. Just ask your animal friend.

Chapter Seven

Talking with Troubled Animals

"My dog is chewing our furniture."

"Our cat is peeing on the carpet."

"My dog barks all the time; how do I stop it?"

TO STOP OR CONTROL animals from doing what *we* don't want them to do is not the answer. Let us look beyond the behavior that is upsetting us and see deeper within the animal's workings.

First, let's look at why there are problems.

Behaviors and habits that we consider inappropriate can develop for any number of reasons. They can be the result of trauma suffered earlier on or can be reactions to our lifestyle and the way we use our energies, directly or indirectly, and how we relate with them. The reasons are often multi-level. I have found that it's important to work with all of these aspects when communicating with an animal. I spend time talking with their person as well in order to get to the bottom of things.

"MY DOG, CHRISTINE, stays outside all day while I work, but why does she jump the fence at times? And when I let her in the house while I'm home, why does she chew objects?"

I asked Christine and she said, "This is how I feel about my life and relationship with my person. Torn apart, shredded, and sad. I'm lonely and bored in the yard all day. When my person is home, she's usually busy moving through the house. She thinks about other things she has to do.

"I'm frustrated and heartbroken. I just want her to give me attention and listen. She never does because she's too busy. I jump the fence because I don't get to run enough. It's also fun and exciting. Besides, she might think I'm running away from home. Maybe she'd pay more attention to me."

Ann ends up chasing after Christine when she jumps fences. Christine receives attention, but not the kind she really wants and needs. When animals don't have needs met, they let us know.

I asked Ann if she set time aside to spend with Christine. Ann responded, "I have a very hectic schedule but I'm home most evenings. When I'm home, I have a lot to do. We do sit on the couch and watch TV sometimes. I talk to her while I do things around the house."

Ann added, "I'm sure she gets plenty of exercise and loves being outside during the day."

Being outdoors all day, as Christine mentioned, gets lonely and boring. Since dogs are very social creatures, they desire to be close to their person or family. Christine was feeling shut out of her person's life.

What I hear again and again from many animals, especially dogs, is "I'm lonely. I feel left out. Everyone is so busy all the time."

Christine isn't a bad dog. She's a normal dog with normal needs. But her anxiety had to surface somehow so she started to jump the fence and chew objects in the house. It also became a way to gain attention. We don't chew objects or jump fences (or most of us don't), but we, too, have ways to be noticed. I told Ann what Christine communicated to me, but she really didn't want to hear.

I suggested Ann run and play with Christine more often. Another important recommendation was for Ann to communicate with Christine verbally and telepathically and for her to be present in mind during these times. This would give them special time together, which would fill Christine's needs and create a more satisfying relationship for both of them.

Ann needed to focus on the relationship rather than on just stopping Christine's chewing and fence jumping. She said she'd try, even though she really didn't have the time to do all that. She asked me if I could do "something" to just stop her bad habits?

I encouraged Ann to take time with Christine so they could build a rewarding relationship. Ann called me several months later to say that Christine was doing better when she took time to be with her.

WHEN UNWANTED HABITS continue for a long time, the animal may find it difficult to give them up. Sound familiar? The intensity of a pattern as well as an animal's personality plays a major role. The behavior pattern or habit impresses itself on the animal's physical, mental, and emotional energy bodies and it becomes like an addiction.

Many dogs telepathically say to me, "I started barking and now I can't stop. I can't help myself." This is when our guidance can assist an animal.

Undesirable habits are encouraged when people visualize and focus their negative feelings on the unwanted behavior. The animals see the pictures in our minds, pick up our feelings, and messages, and think, *That's what they want me to do*. The habit continues or may even get worse.

RITA IS A VERY NICE but scattered woman. "My dog barks when I'm gone, and sometimes when I'm here. My neighbors complain and I don't know what to do. Why is he barking? What can you do to make him stop?"

Rita also mentioned that Monroe was very protective of the family.

I asked her questions about her home life, schedule, and personal life. It's important to hear both the person's and animal's point of view. This allows me to get an overall picture of my animal client's household.

I asked Monroe to communicate about his barking. "I was told to be a watchdog and protect our territory. I bark to keep trespassers out. My person shows me mental pictures of myself barking."

I asked why he barked when Rita was home. He revealed a picture to me of her yelling at him while he barked. Then I saw a flash of hands wrapped around Monroe's throat choking him. Barking got him attention, but not in a positive way.

Before I told Rita what Monroe conveyed to me, Rita said, "I worry about him barking during the day. If he barks when I get home, I get real irritated and tell him to shut up. I could just choke him."

When I heard her words, my heart hit the ground. Monroe was receiving Rita's mental images of choking him. So he barked even more.

Monroe's barking habit was difficult for him too, because he couldn't stop. He barked because of the mental images she sent him, and because he was frustrated and confused, caught between Rita's contradictory messages.

How was he expected to act? Rita wanted him to be a "silent watchdog." She didn't want him to bark at friends or neighbors but only at suspicious-looking strangers around or in the house. This is unrealistic, since a dog's natural way to alert the family and defend their property is to bark.

Monroe needed to know exactly what Rita expected of him. He was open and eager and waiting for her to be clear.

I suggested some ways Rita could guide Monroe. "Correct him from a centered place while he's barking rather than resisting his barking. Praise him immediately when he quiets down. This way he experiences good feelings and your attention in positive ways.

"You can feel the difference between acting from your clear, non-emotional centered self or from resistant feelings. Resisting and getting tense feeds the barking." Rita started to understand the difference. "When he quiets down, stroke and praise him in a calm, peaceful manner." Peaceful and positive feelings are essential because they are alive and fill our mental images with power that can transform old patterns. I suggested that she send Monroe clear images of the behavior she desired from him. I asked her to remember to be realistic with expectations, but to also expect the best.

Rita spent extra time playing with Monroe (which he requested), and telepathically explained to him what actions she desired from him.

Monroe's barking greatly lessened, but at times, when Rita slips into old patterns, so does Monroe.

MARION CALLED AND ASKED why her dog Tammy barked at men. I asked, "How are you feeling toward men?"

She laughed and said, "I guess I don't trust them very much."

Tammy communicated with me saying, "She told me to be a watchdog and I am a good watchdog. I guard the house, territory, and her, just like she wants me to. It is my duty and I am proud of doing a good job, especially when men come to the house. If I bark at them, they don't come so close to our territory. I know my person feels angry at men. When she does, I bark for her."

After Marion and I talked, she became aware that she had given Tammy unspoken messages to be a watchdog, especially in regard to men.

She had moved to the country and was afraid of being alone. Marion had unconsciously asked Tammy to protect her and the place. To protect means to bark.

Marion chose to deal with her personal issues so Tammy wouldn't continue to act them out.

Tammy is now more relaxed and doesn't bark the way she used to at friends or other men as they approach the house.

Resolving Issues

AT TIMES, when I do a consultation for someone, I may end up doing more work with them than with their animal friend.

Sometimes it can be difficult for a person to alter their habits. If an animal is doing well at breaking a habit, but the person continues to affect an animal because of their attitudes and issues, the animal finds it difficult to maintain new ways.

But other times, animals might continue bad habits if they get some kind of emotional payoff from it. The payoff is often attention. "Stop that barking right now, or else," or "Oh, poor baby, let mama hold you."

When animals discover that an unwanted habit doesn't get them attention anymore, they often drop the habit if they get attention and praise for more desirable behavior. The animal begins to get the message if the person is telepathically sending what is desired. Also, an animal should get positive attention, like stroking, for cooperating, putting forth effort to change, and finally making the change that is really best for them. (Best meaning constructive rather than destructive habits for both animal and person. Humans judge what is good or bad for their animal and so it's important to consider and cooperate with animals' natural ways, especially since they don't think in terms of good and bad behavior.)

Misbehaviors are often symptoms of unseen issues on deeper levels. Listen to and talk with your animal to discern the key source of her actions. See things from the animal's point of view. What is the animal saying through his or her behavior? Animals have reasons and intentions behind their actions.

Just punishing or correcting an animal's outer symptoms won't heal deeper emotional problems. The same or different patterns will pop up later. What manifests as a physical ailment may enter the scene. A number of physical problems can be symptoms of unresolved turmoil. (I always make sure the person takes the animal to a veterinarian before we work together. This way we know if there is a specific physical problem, and find out if or how it is connected to an emotional issue.)

MOST ANIMALS ARE WILLING and can choose to redirect undesirable habits. Animals are very capable of making change; and therefore, we need to believe and trust in their natural intelligence and abilities.

If we are in touch with our inner Self, we can connect with the animal's essence and use inner eyes, ears, and heart to understand the animal. Then reshaping and shifting the energy of habit patterns can take place so as to emphasize the more positive actions for the animal. (Remember, habits are energy patterns.)

The decision to alter habits must be mutual, on some level, between animal and person. If either animal or person is resistant or unsure, they cannot effectively flow in true harmony. Let the animal know telepathically that she has a choice to act from her center or inner Self rather than in reaction to circumstances. The energy of the habitual pattern can then shift in a way that helps create change on the physical level. This automatically moves the animal away from the unwanted habit. It is an in-depth, subtle, silent way of showing the animal that she has alternatives to old habits.

When I work with animals at this deep level, I connect with their spirit. Connecting with and encouraging their spirit brings out their potential, which cuts through and goes beyond conditioning and habits. Like people, they tend to get lost in emotions and outer circumstances. Yet their core or spirit is wise and aware, and desires productive ways to express their best qualities.

In this way, we can guide animals back into balance. But we must first be in balance. Animals can be out of balance because we are out of balance.

People often want immediate changes in their animal friend and this can happen. It depends on how ingrained the habit or behavior is, and also on what the person's attitudes and beliefs are.

Many people tell me they see shifts take place in their animal companion during and right after a consultation.

Patience is as precious as gold when an animal is opening to new ways of acting and being.

If a habit persists, then some significant stone has been left unturned.

Obedience Education (Training)

OBEDIENCE EDUCATION can help an animal develop her potential if done correctly and with love. The first step is to get the animal's undivided attention. That can take patience and persuasion. Animals feel scared and unsure about changes and challenges just as we do. If the animal's mind isn't present and focused on her person, then she's not listening.When the animal feels comfortable in class, she can then be shown positive ways to make choices and to express herself.

The person must stay within his own center, yet blend with or sense the animal's body energies. One can imagine the leash to be the energy connection between the person and the animal. Actually, the person's intentions do flow through the leash. Then they can gently guide her on a leash through movements, while showing her pictures of desired actions.

This can change groove-like reactions. For example, if you think and feel the desire to walk, your intention causes the body's energy to want to move in that direction. The animal perceives the flow and has the choice to follow and flow with the intention, or to resist, react, and go her own way. The more the animal can flow and soften, the easier it is for everyone, but the person must initially be the one who is flexible in order to be totally present with the animal.

The person must keep in mind that energy takes whatever shape, form, and quality we give it. It is easy to see the harmony and unity when a person and animal blend in movement. This is an efficient, harmonious way to guide and show an animal that they can sometimes make better choices for themselves. It's important to respect and honor the animal at all times.

By using positive guidance and reinforcement, the animal's mind develops more fully and can learn how to think more clearly and make better, more constructive decisions. This way of guiding helps an animal to resolve conflict.

Each animal is different. Differences in temperament and timing must be considered. Balance, flexibility, and sensitivity are necessary when showing animals different ways to resolve out-of-balance actions. Also, the person needs to be willing to negotiate with the animal companion so both the animal and person are happy with what's going on. Equally significant is for the animal's person to look at their reactions to the animal in order to discover what energies would be helpful to redirect.

Insecurities

A COMMON SOURCE of problems in animals is insecurity. Insecurity wears many masks. Kennel animals, former strays, abused animals, and those passed from home to home often display a variety of insecurity problems. A dog educator called me to consult with him on a case involving a dog, Leo, who was born in a kennel. I was told he was aggressive and running his humans' household. In three years, he had bitten the husband twice, the wife and fourteen-year-old son once. Leo had never attempted to bite anyone else. Currently, he was in obedience education. As I entered their home, I felt thick tension that hung in the air around the threesome. All three started shouting rather than talking about Leo. They laughed while telling me, all at the same time, stories about Leo's growling and biting episodes. And the son, who was trying to shout over his parents, bellowed out that he wrestled a lot with Leo when he was a puppy. They all seemed proud and delighted about having what they termed an aggressive, biting dog. It became clear to me that the constant chatter and laughter hid unexpressed anger they felt toward each other. "Sometimes when Leo sits on my lap," laughed the man, "I start to get up from the chair and he growls and won't let me up. Then my wife gets something to distract him so I can get up." Leo would threaten them every few weeks by growling, snapping, or firmly grabbing one of their wrists. A leash was attached to his collar so one of them could grab it if Leo started to growl. Leo was now running the household. I asked Leo to share his side of the story. He jumped onto my lap, licked my face, and sat down beside me.

"I'm the center of attention and I'm going to get all of it. I know they're afraid of me. If they hit me, I still get all the attention. I run the household and I like it." When I heard this, I wondered what had created this way of thinking, so I asked him to tell me more. "When I was very young I had playmates at the kennel. I had to bully my way with them. I wasn't as big or strong as some of the others."

Leo's experiences had created and encouraged uncertainty in him at a young, impressionable age. Leo's source of insecurity was really his fear of being pushed around, so he pushed first. He didn't want to be the underdog. Leo went on, "My people make constant emotional demands on me that they really need to have filled by each other. I feel like I'm in the middle of a tug-of-war."

Leo is greatly overloaded by his family's hidden turmoils. "No one believes I am good. I want to please, but I must act this way to maintain control. I get very tired. They expect me to bite and run the household. They have never understood me and don't give me a chance to be myself. How else can I be? I've tried to let the biting go, really. I've become set in this way." Leo didn't know how else to act.

Leo let me know his family was driving him crazy with loud voices, fears, frustrations, and unexpressed angers, all of which he was absorbing. The family's fear-filled attitudes and images of Leo biting them perpetuated his way of being. From time to time he went off like a time bomb because he had few opportunities to really exercise, which would have let him release some tension.

In one way, Leo was getting what he wanted—attention. He was adept at keeping his family in place. What an energy-draining front and position to maintain.

Leo is a scapegoat for the family and is regarded as the "family problem." This was a family affair since Leo had never tried to bite anyone else. They continually talked about and focused on his problem.

I proposed Leo continue his obedience education. Here he could experience himself in new ways and learn who he is. The main problem was going back home because of the way his family related to him. This could cause Leo to slip back into old patterns.

This family did not deal directly with Leo, and wanted the dog educator to "get rid" of his aggression. Ideally, one of the family would have worked with the educator and dog. Through him, they could have learned who this animal was and how to confront their own issues in a direct way.

By showing Leo, gently and firmly yet softly, other ways to act and how to deal with stressful situations that trigger aggression, he'll learn to respond from inner security and confidence. (Leo's bullying stemmed from insecurity.)

The woman thought about this and decided to give it a try. She worked with Leo in dog obedience, and his patterns started to change. But the husband wasn't willing to accept that his attitudes were affecting Leo. However, the family is looking at their interactions with each other and that is a positive step. Leo was glad they were making an effort.

GENERALLY, IF ANIMALS have lived with us since birth or an early age, we have had a great influence in shaping and understanding them. When a stray animal knocks at our door and becomes a family member, it's a different story. Fortunately, telepathic communication can answer many questions and help to bridge gaps about animals that come our way.

Tim and Mark adopted three stray cats that paraded into their yard, their hearts, and their household, all within three months.

They wanted to know the cats' backgrounds as well as their feelings about living with each other. Chuck and Toby were adjusting well before Andy entered the scene. Toby began spraying, and Chuck offered a contribution or two of his own. Andy told me he sprayed just once but then felt bad about it.

Chuck, Toby, and Andy, each in their own unique way, have shared insecurities though communications. The three felines showed me pieces of their lives since birth. Their accounts show why stray animals often feel insecure and how insecurities are revealed through various actions.

CHUCK, A BRIGHT ORANGE TIGER, began, "I was taken from my mother when young. Not a pleasant experience. I was given to a neighbor with kids and they grabbed and pulled at me so I decided to go outside more often. People threw things at me when they caught me in their garbage. My people were thinking about moving and I wasn't sure I wanted to go. And the day they moved they could not find me. When I went to the house, it was empty. I got hungry and thirsty so had to find a new home.

"Now I am with new people. I don't like to be smothered but I do want affection. Sometimes they don't really smother me, but I remember those kids and haven't gotten over that experience. I prefer to be with adults."

When Mark and Tim leave town on business for a few days, Chuck reacts and says, "I'm concerned they might leave or oust me out of the house." This worry can be seen in his actions and comes from being left behind by the family, even though he wasn't sure he wanted to go with them.

Chuck also gets very jealous when Toby and Andy get attention. His response is, "I was here first. I want attention but don't want the others to see that I need it."

"Is there enough space in this house for all of us cats? [Tim and Mark live in a huge house.] I think the house is too small." This was Chuck's perspective because of his insecurities.

Communicating with Chuck, Toby, and Andy allowed them to release pent-up feelings. The cats were happy to know someone would listen.

When bottled-up animals first converse and realize a human hears them, they can ventilate strong, intense feelings and thoughts. Like a cork popping out of a bottle, pressure gets released and everything pours out. About halfway through the conversation, the animal's energy softens and they communicate with a more even-tempered flow.

TOBY, A WHITE FELINE, started his story with strong feeling. "I felt I was in the way. There was a lot of arguing among a man and woman and two children. I wandered outside more and more. One day the man kicked me out. I really do not like humans. It's hard for me to trust and accept them. I feel safer around other animals.

"Chuck tries to appear big when he feels I'm in his territory. I appear aloof and do things in other ways to Chuck that humans never notice."

As the communication progresses Toby's energy softens. "Well, I really do care about my people," he says. "They fed and cared for me during hard times. I'm afraid of feeling too much and showing them too much of what I feel.

"Chuck thinks I'm bigger than he is; I am. Andy thinks he's very little but he's not."

Toby moves into discussing earlier, painful times.

"I was born under a house by a porch where it was cold and damp. I remember staying close to my warm mother. It was hard to stay alive. My mother was hungry and tired when she gave birth to us. When I was very young someone gave me to the family I mentioned. I hated being taken from Mother. I felt sick for a long time because I deeply missed her. I don't like to talk about my past. Humans have some things to prove to me. Things were going pretty well with Chuck and me until Andy came along. I had to mark my territory because who knows how many cats might come to live here.

"I know I can get more attention from my people if I leave the house for a long time or lift my leg. They think of me. I know Tim and Mark worry about me, which I like. No one else has ever cared.

"Tell my people I hear them call for me, but I don't want to go to the house when they want me to. I try to respect their wishes but get distracted and moody at times."

As Toby himself mentioned, what he communicates to Chuck and Andy is very subtle. He is slick, smooth, and a master of the streetwise games he had to play to survive.

ANDY IS EXTREMELY INSECURE due to his past. One day after living with Mark and Tim for over eight months, he suddenly scratched Mark and whirled around like a tornado onto the porch. As Mark ran over and opened the porch door, Andy flew up into the attic.

I asked Andy what had happened. "I saw a man coming towards me and thought he was going to take a swing at me with the stick he was carrying. I knew it was really Mark, but reacted because it reminded me of something from long ago. A man who didn't like cats swung and hit me with a stick for sniffing through his garbage. All I saw was the big stick, which was bigger than me." (Mark was holding an umbrella).

"Sometimes I'm overwhelmed with scared feelings and want to run, but I don't know what I'm running from. Maybe from those in my past.

"Everybody is bigger than me. I have always felt tiny and lost." Andy was very concerned about his body, and that he might not survive. "I wasn't wanted so I left at an early age and lived on the streets for a while. I stayed with a woman who later died. And here I am with my people.

"I have learned how to attract humans. Don't you think I'm cute? Tim and Mark think so. But I still feel insecure and unloved at times. I try and make myself big like Chuck and Toby.

"I feel I'm exposing myself by telling you this. Please don't tell my people; they may kick me out.

"I have it good here. I don't feel like I deserve such a wonderful home. Maybe I should be on the street again. No, I love the comfort and this house.

"I guess Chuck and Toby really are pretty good cats even though troublesome at times. I'm getting used to them. Please don't give me away."

It was obvious Andy had inner conflicts concerning his image.

Andy's concern about the consequences of exposing himself isn't unusual. Toby had the same concern and was upset with me because he knew I could see his thoughts.

I reassured them that Mark and Tim would understand and that I felt it best to tell them what they had told me to enable better understanding between them. After telling them this, they agreed it was okay for me to pass their thoughts on.

Some animals don't want me to tell their thoughts because it will ruin a game they are playing. For example, a dog in obedience school might tell me she doesn't want to do what's expected and acts dumb because her people think she's dumb anyway. But this is not the usual case.

All three cats were greatly affected by their backgrounds. Chuck needs his space respected because of his previous encounter with children. He becomes jealous when unsure about his position as top cat. Toby has trouble trusting humans and does not allow himself to be open, direct, or vulnerable. Andy perceives himself as smaller than he really is. He gets scared when someone approaches him with stick-like objects and flips into flashbacks: a case of post-traumatic stress disorder.

But after talking with the three of them, they were all more open and secure. They are closer with Tim and Mark and each other. Insecurities still pop out, but isn't that true for all of us?

Animals Dealing with Issues

I ENCOURAGE ANIMALS to discuss painful experiences, so they can then release them.

Andy's horrible experience of a man swinging a stick at him was one of those times.

Andy and I sat on the floor face to face. After some casual telepathic conversation, I asked him to tell me more about this particular experience. His reply was, "I don't want to talk about it." On that note, he stood up, turned tail, and headed for the door. Andy did not want to remember the pain that remained wrapped up in this traumatic event.

If he chose to share the great fear he had felt, it would lose its hold over him. He could better live and act from the present.

Andy finally showed me a few fragments from the event. I could feel what he had felt, as though he would die from fright and a big stick.

Sharing this with me allowed him to release some of the terror. Next, I sent gentle, loving energy to Andy, along with his guardian angels to help heal the old wounds.

I send sincere loving feelings to all animals after communicating with them. One way takes the form of surrounding them with beautiful golden light. Golden light is energy that heals and lets them know I care. I end all sessions by thanking them and sending them peace and love.

When working with animals like Andy, I apologize for thoughtless, ignorant humans who have hurt them so deeply. I convey that all humans don't act in such ways.

Another time, I asked Andy to show me, through his eyes, how he saw Chuck and Toby. I saw two huge cats, twice their actual size.

Andy's inner being was so squashed down, he perceived Chuck and Toby as bigger than life. Through mental pictures I showed Andy their true body sizes because I wanted him to see them as they really are.

I also showed Andy his actual size. He could see he was a big cat. (He is.) This gave him a different perspective from which to view himself and the others. He thought about this for quite a while.

Andy's letting go of the pain a bit at a time, as humans do. He is now more confident, connected to himself. This can be seen in the ways he relates to Chuck, Toby, and his people.

In cases such as these, I often do Soul Recovery Work (see chapter 12).

MARGE CONTACTED ME about her cat Danny, a stray who hung around her house for weeks before allowing her to approach him. He had been surviving in the woods nearby for a long time. She would leave food in the garage for him since he only ate when everyone disappeared. (She had two cats and three dogs.) As time passed Danny seemed to grow accustomed to Marge.

Danny developed an eye infection. A veterinarian treated the eye, and since they were there she decided to have him neutered. Marge brought him home and placed him in a spare room. (He had never been in the house.) After he healed, Marge let him out of the room to mix with the other animals.

"He attacked my cats several times so I isolated him in my bedroom and he has been living in there for seven months," she said. "I was afraid he might injure one of the cats. He's like a kamikaze. Whenever I open the bedroom door, he's ready to pounce and destroy any unfortunate cat around. I have him on a leash and he trots with me to the door if other cats are not around. I use the leash to occasionally take him outside but he wants to attack any cats passing by.

"If the other cats are outside, I let Danny roam the house."

When I asked Danny about his actions I could feel his conflict. He was full of highly charged, jumbled feelings. He was wound up like a tight ball of string. "I've had to be aggressive to survive. Humans mistreated me and I've been in tough scraps with cats."

Danny showed me telepathically the trauma and inner turmoil of being neutered and put into a room, all in one day. He had just begun to trust Marge and *wham!* One day he's free; the next day he's shut up in a strange house and in a room he's never seen, and feeling pain. It was almost more than he could bear.

Concerning his current life in the bedroom, he said sadly, "I feel forlorn, bored, lonely, and confined. Want to be out of here and don't. I don't understand why they don't accept my behavior. Why am I separated from other cats? I just do what I've always had to do to survive."

Being shut up in a room was creating more aggression and fear in Danny. Marge told him the other cats would live with him in peace if he didn't act so "barbaric." Danny couldn't understand her feelings, or those of the other cats. Marge and the room became his security.

I communicated to Danny saying, "You can act differently with these cats and survive. They are not like cats you tangled with in the woods." Through mental images, I showed him how he could interact with them. Danny's response was, "I feel unsafe and vulnerable. I don't know how to fit in."

Danny had never learned how to fit into the social structure and culture of house cats. As a result, he attacks from fear in order to survive.

Danny needed to get out of that room, out of seclusion. I suggested that Marge let him out of the bedroom while on a leash to roam around the house. Also, to walk him outside so he could observe the other cats from a safe distance.

Another factor that invited Danny's aggression was that Marge was afraid her cats would be injured by Danny. Her image of Danny being a "kamikaze, barbaric destroyer" was only making circumstances more difficult.

Marge was aware she needed to deal with her fearful feelings and images about aggression so as not to encourage Danny's pattern of striking before thinking.

Danny would get aggressive because he knew everyone around him got scared—cats and people. If he could scare the cats they would stay away, and he would survive. Aggression was the only way to survive. How could he let down his guard?

Marge's patience and support, along with some suggestions I gave her, allowed Danny to change his attitude step by step and stop threatening the others.

Caring and commitment are important when an animal with Danny's background is trying to cope with so many sudden, unfamiliar adjustments. Empathy, guidance, support, and respect inspire an animal to feel more secure and to grow beyond old habits.

Danny now spends as much time as he wishes enjoying the outside. Marge puts an elastic leash on him and attaches it to a long line so he can move about almost the entire yard. When the other cats are inside, he has complete freedom off the leash. Things continue to progress with all of them.

Elimination Misbehavior

When animals leave their calling cards—urine and fecal material—in the house or outside of their litter pans, they are communicating a message (not usually including puppies or sick animals).

Animals urinate or defecate in the house for a variety of reasons. The animal may be acting out their person's unexpressed feelings, or there may be some misunderstanding the animal is trying to tell their person about. The animal could be stating how she feels toward a person or situation.

Marion was concerned about her neutered cat Tony ever since her lover, Douglas, had moved into her house. Tony was consistently defecating on Douglas's pillow.

Douglas had permanently moved into Tony's sleeping place next to his mistress.

Douglas made it clear to Marion he did not like cats and called them "nuisances," and Tony got the message loud and clear.

Tony's response, on the pillow, told Douglas in clear terms how he felt about his presence in the house, and more specifically, about his sleeping place. Tony wanted Douglas "eliminated" from the house, his life, and his relationship with Marion. Tony was also fulfilling Douglas's expectations about cats. What he expected, he received. This also was a time of adjustment for Marion. She was feeling uncertain about the new arrangement and concerned over Douglas's attitudes toward cats, reinforcing Tony's behavior.

When I asked Tony about his actions he commented, "I hope this expression of marking my territory discourages that man from sleeping in my place."

Fortunately, Douglas was willing to view cats in a more positive way. As he began to adopt different attitudes, he and Tony began accepting each other.

Marion and Douglas finally settled into the new circumstances. So did Tony. He stopped leaving messages on Douglas's pillow and Tony now sleeps on the sheets with his mistress and her mister.

Digging and Chewing

OTHER COMMON ISSUES are digging holes and chewing household items. Many animals communicate to me they chew and dig out of boredom and frustration as a means of releasing pent-up feelings.

Some dogs dig because they are lonely and separated from their person who works long hours. When their people are home, they aren't given enough attention or allowed in the house for long, so the animal feels left out.

While I was receiving calls on a radio show one evening, a woman phoned in and said, "I have a huge backyard for my dog Gretta to play in all day. I know she loves it, but she digs holes and I don't know why.

"One day while cleaning the house I heard banging. I hurried into my family room where the sound was coming from. Gretta was standing up with paws pressed against the window. She looked like she was trying to get in so I went outside to see what was wrong, but no one was around. She's been doing this more often. What's wrong with her?"

I asked Gretta about digging and pressing against the window. She communicated frustration, boredom, and sadness because her person constantly put her outside. Don't we want to be close to the most important people in our lives?

The woman couldn't believe Gretta desperately wanted to be close to her. She couldn't imagine Gretta, her dog, had emotional needs. The woman commented, "Animals want to be outside. They belong outside most of the time."

Dogs need social contact and sense when they aren't included as an important part of a family.

Some animals do prefer being outside most of the time, but for the most part, we have bred dogs to depend on humans for their mental, physical, and emotional well-being. Playing in a yard alone doesn't fill their basic needs.

ONE DELIGHTFUL DOG named Chet lives with Tammy and Dick. He was chewing up important business papers, Kleenex, and other household items.

I asked Chet to explain why he chewed. He responded, "It keeps my mind and body occupied when no one is here. I'm active and need to be active. If someone would play with me more, I wouldn't get into other things. I just can't help myself when I chew, but when I chew I get attention. I love it! My people are always coming and going and I'm left alone."

Chet brought an important point to my attention. His people have loud arguments on a regular basis, which is another reason for his chewing. Chet also added, "The woman talks so loud it hurts my ears and eyes at times and I don't know how to tell her to talk quietly. Tell her I can hear her whisper. The noise they both make hurts my ears and makes me feel sad, nervous, and confused. I'm torn between them and don't know which one to go to to comfort because I love both."

I could sense Chet's emotional and physical dilemma. His mind and body didn't know which way to go when he heard arguing. He felt forlorn.

Furthermore, any subconscious thoughts the couple threw at each other like darts created just as real a turmoil for Chet. In his own way, by chewing and tearing papers apart, Chet was showing them what they do to him and each other.

Many animals express to me how deeply they are affected by people arguing. Loud voices and intense emotions that fly around and fill a house cause chaos and stress for the animal, sometimes affecting body and mind. Unfortunately, animals usually have no escape from this kind of energy.

I suggested to Chet's people that before they argue they let him outside or argue in a different room. (This depends on the individual animal's reactions.) Also, I proposed that one of them explain the arguing was not about or directed at him. Some animals think arguments involve them. If a person has yelled at the animal with a similar tone they can think it's directed at them. It's important to make it clear that they are not the cause of conflict, just as parents would hopefully do with a young child.

Tammy and Dick would be very upset when they'd come home and find chewed objects. They were reprimanding Chet, which got him "big" attention. I asked them to ignore what he had chewed and to be neutral about looking at or focusing on the object. Also, to give Chet the same welcome whether he had chewed something or not. When they did this, Chet quickly realized chewing wasn't going to get him anything.

It's important to know the source of an animal's misdirected behavior. The animal, with guidance, can then begin to rechannel digging/chewing (or whatever) energy in a different direction. Simply to focus on getting rid of the symptoms won't resolve deeper emotional issues.

Plenty of exercise and playtime are necessary. They are good ways to release frustration. Otherwise, pent-up energies get misdirected into chewing, digging, or other nervous habits. Exercise doesn't solve everything, but it helps. Playtime adds a spontaneous, joyful flow and connection between person and animal that is fulfilling.

Another aspect of Chet's problem is that he's scattered. His mind moves in a hundred directions at once. When I conversed with Chet, his thoughts were everywhere. It took every ounce of his concentration to listen to my questions. The woman said he had been through obedience training. I told her Chet knew what he kind-of-had-to-do outwardly to please and get praise, but most of the time he wasn't focused or present.

I suggested some of the techniques mentioned earlier in this chapter about obedience education. If Chet could develop his ability to think and concentrate, he could focus his attention on his people when asked. With such guidance, Chet could alter his scattered way of being.

Tammy began to play and exercise more with Chet and also toned down her voice. Since Tammy and John live in a small house, it's difficult to argue without Chet being practically on top of them, but when they argue they explain to Chet that he isn't part of it nor responsible for comforting them.

Overall, Chet's chewing of household items has greatly decreased. Chet's people understand the causes and continue to strive toward resolving their issues.

HERE IS ANOTHER example of how arguing can effect an animal. One woman tells me her calico cat, Mocha, stands between her and her husband yowling when they yell during heated arguments. I asked Mocha about it. "Arguing makes me feel sick. The noise hurts me. The intensity and force of the energy is difficult to handle. I get between them to voice how I feel. I want them to stop. It scares me and it's painful to feel that energy travel through me, and them."

Depression

A WHITE MARE, Pearl, had been purchased by Miranda for her fifteen-year-old daughter Peggy. Pearl showed great potential as a show horse until she went lame.

The daughter started showing another horse and leaving Pearl behind. Miranda and Peggy wanted me to find out how Pearl's leg felt and why she seemed so depressed.

The minute I saw Pearl, she began transmitting a deep sadness to me. It was overwhelming. She leaned her head against my shoulder and began pouring out her heart. "No one listens or pays attention to me anymore. I've been replaced and I am depressed.

"My leg still bothers me. I worry about it and I'm scared to run and jump."

Later on I sent her a mental picture of herself using the leg normally but wisely. Pearl was overly fearful about using her leg. She thought if she exercised in a normal way, she would get hurt. I wanted her to know that that needn't be true.

Pearl continued, "My heart has never been in shows or winning. It doesn't matter to me. I miss the attention and seeing other horses, but performing isn't important. I love to run and be free more than anything, and I'd be content to have my peoples' attention, browse in fields, and feel like I belong."

When I shared Pearl's thoughts with Miranda and Peggy they cried, and so did I.

Miranda spoke through tears saying, "Both of us began to neglect her after she went lame and we feel very guilty. We started shutting her out more and more, which made things worse. I knew she was sad and I guess I knew why, but I just couldn't face it."

Pearl was watching us from her stall and it was healing for her to see them and hear them say it aloud. They were accepting their true feelings for the first time. "Pearl was a major disappointment," said Miranda. This sensitive horse had picked up her thought. When Pearl could no longer be worked or shown, mother and daughter withdrew from her emotionally even though they took care of her physical needs.

Pearl's depression could have been minimized had they expressed their feelings with her. With everything in the open, their guilt would have dissipated and they would have related to Pearl differently. The guilt created walls; more guilt resulted in more walls.

Pearl had every reason to feel dejected and depressed. Lameness set up the situation, but her people's reactions brought on the deeper depression.

I suggested that Miranda and Peggy have honest talks with Pearl to straighten things out. This would open channels for good feelings to flow to Pearl. I recommended they send the flow gradually since Pearl might feel overwhelmed by the sudden tidal wave of good feelings sent her way.

After Pearl and I communicated she sighed and said, "I feel much better. I'm so glad they know how I feel, and I see how they feel."

Shortly after I saw Pearl her depression lifted. She started moving about the field as she had before going lame.

Let Us Listen

AS MENTIONED EARLIER, chewing, urinating, and other off-balance habits an animal develops are often the results of frustrations, fears, and feelings that need to come out somewhere. Other signs of frustration or unhappiness can be spotted if an animal is depressed or ill. These red light alert messages are telling us to stop, look, and listen.

The energy animals use to dig up yards, defecate on beds, and so on can be redirected once they know they are heard, noticed, and understood. Of course, the source of the problem must first be addressed, and then it can be resolved.

The source of the symptoms may exist within the animal, their people, or both. Other people and circumstances may play a role.

Just correcting the animal's symptoms doesn't work for long because the problem will emerge in a different way.

We can learn significant lessons from and about our animal friends by telepathically communicating with them. We may not understand everything, but we will know more than if we never try to connect. Heart-to-heart communication is the fundamental key and at the very core of understanding our animal companions and why they do what they do. Communication benefits both person and animal, which then enhances the relationship at every level.

Chapter Eight

Animals in Our Zoos

I HAD NUMEROUS conversations with different gorillas at zoos over the years. At the beginning of my communications, most gorillas were existing in small, separate cages. One male lowland gorilla named Arthur silently told me that people staring at him greatly affected him because there was nowhere to get away. He was frustrated and depressed.

I learned a great deal about gorillas as well as from them. Arthur nonverbally taught me there are many layers to animals, and that each layer has its own purpose. He showed me the image of peeling an onion and told me to learn about the different layers. Then he took me beyond the layers and showed me his center, or true spiritual self.

This creature felt hopeless and angry during the many years he had been kept in a cage. Very often he would beat his chest and rush toward the bars at visitors as a way of expressing frustration and discharging pent-up energy.

One day, early in our relationship, I was looking directly at him with my fingers covering most of my eyes. (Gorillas don't like to be stared at because they interpret it as a threat.) The message he shot over to me was, "I know you're looking at me whether or not you cover your eyes." Was I ever embarrassed!

Arthur went on to say, "People see themselves in me. They project their fears and other things they don't want to accept about themselves onto me: shadowy fears of their own wildness. Yet they are attracted to me, to their primal urges."

This handsome gorilla communicated that he often regurgitated his food because of boredom. (This is a problem with gorillas kept in cages.) He silently said his body ached and felt stiff from the cold concrete floors.

"There's nothing to take up the time. Will I always just walk around in a cage? Being in a cage diminishes many of my abilities. There's no reason to develop my abilities because I'm just existing." He let me know through mental pictures that he was in communication with gorillas who were in the outdoor exhibits. He couldn't understand why be couldn't be with them.

But his life and that of other gorillas has improved greatly. This sensitive creature is now much happier tumbling about on green grass outside in a larger natural exhibit area with other gorillas. The change in him has been dramatic. He feels like life is worth living now. His spirit is joyful. He is healing.

Zoo Environment

MANY ANIMALS are greatly affected by their surroundings, so it is important to simulate their natural environment as much as possible. Even though the natural exhibits are a big improvement in zoos, however, they are not the same as being in the wild. The zoos do the best they can.

The animals communicate that they need quiet and private areas away from staring people. A number of animals, especially those in the children's zoo areas, tell me they enjoy visitors, but sometimes feel extremely drained when there is too much physical contact.

Orcas, dolphins, and seals who are confined in what seem to us to be large pools often do not enjoy their lives the way they would if they were in the sea with their families.

Noise, air pollution, and peoples' chatter and thoughts bombard the animals, assaulting their whole being. Sometimes there's nowhere they can go to get away from it all. Animals are born with innate urges to move their bodies in natural ways, and if they can't do this because of limited space, they experience frustration. Some animals get sick or even die, and some animals appear to be vicious because of their living conditions.

Zoo visitors love to relate to the animals, but the animals' needs should be considered first and foremost. Zookeepers do a great deal in caring for the animals.

Many animals tell me telepathically how much they dislike people pointing at them, chasing them, or laughing at them. Loud screaming hurts not only their ears, but their entire bodies. Some of the animals also communicate that they feel the love and joy that people send to them from their hearts.

Today, zoos' educational programs are teaching children how to correctly handle and care for wild animals. Hopefully the children will put into action what they are learning for the sake of all species and the Earth.

One of the saddest animals I've ever met was a bear who was kept in a small private zoo. He was existing in a round pen that wasn't much bigger than he was. This huge grizzly had been used in a hit movie and had been declawed and defanged. When I entered his pen he was friendly. He communicated that he liked being outdoors, but hated not having any room to move around in. The people who had purchased him didn't realize how hard it was on him to live in such a small enclosure, but they had taken him in order to save his life.

Taking animals out of their natural environment is very hard on them. They lose their connection to what is natural and life-giving. But zoos do the best they can in creating the most natural environment they can for the animals. Some animals build defenses in order to deal with living in captivity. Others develop neurotic behaviors that reflect what is happening to them. Some animals are locked away in buildings because there is no room in an exhibit or because they have some other problem. In these instances, the animals feel they have no hope. They may be scared and lonely. Animals in zoos communicate to me that the most common problems are boredom, nervousness, and depression.

Many are trying to help preserve wildlife. Does preserving wild creatures in zoos genuinely benefit them? Do we preserve them because we value them for themselves? We know that what is happening to the animals and the land will eventually happen to us. My intention is not to judge. These are simply questions we might want to ask ourselves.

Zookeepeers

MOST PEOPLE DON'T THINK of animals in zoos having needs that go beyond food and water, yet they do.

Most zookeepers develop close relationships with the animals they care for. They respect them and want what's best for them. I have taught some zookeepers how to telepathically connect with animals and how to apply various holistic techniques to alleviate stress, and to strengthen an animal's overall state of well-being. Most noticed positive changes in the animals and in their relationships with them. Zookeepers work in frustrating circumstances because of the many demands placed on them. Yet they are in a unique position to care for the many species of the world's ambassadors.

Spiritual Perspective

FROM A SPIRITUAL PERSPECTIVE, animals in zoos are special good-will ambassadors for their species. They bring us back in touch with our roots, and reawaken our memories of oneness with all living beings and the source of life itself.

Captive animals help us realize that their species and native lands are fading away. These beings in animal form are our teachers. They have agreed on a soul level to be ambassadors, willing to educate us. Let us treat them with respect and dignity.

A lion told me, "From the personality level, it is difficult to endure pain and limitations through human domination, but on a spiritual level we are all involved in the same spiral of life, of spiritual evolution. Those in human form are becoming aware of this truth."

One wise whale informed me that souls in human form are learning to flow with the natural rhythm of life, to let go of possessing and controlling things. Many other animals have learned this and are living a lifetime of "being" rather than one filled with ego concerns of always "getting" and "doing." The cetacean continued, "We cannot and do not desire or need to control or possess Nature's forms. We have evolved in ways that allow us to trust the spirit within ourselves and in all creation. Humans need to know their spirit and senses, rather than getting lost in control and manipulation."

Each species has its own unique gifts and stories to offer us. Let us listen to the different species before they vanish from the face of the Earth, never to exist in the same form again.

A giraffe in a zoo said this about humans. "Most humans really do not see or hear our messages. Or if they do, they tune them out. It's as though our messages hit a brick wall and bounce off. Most people think all chimps or giraffes or other undomestic species look alike and act the same. No. Every animal is different and unique, as is every human. Children often sense what animals feel. They understand because they aren't yet caught in false beliefs."

Bear Friend

ONE FAMILY FOUND a bear cub sitting along a highway out West. They picked her up and brought her to a zoo. When I looked into her eyes, it was love at first sight.

We became friends during her stay at the zoo. She was being kept in a good-sized pen with green grass and a barrel to hide in and play on. The first time I asked her what she was feeling, her response was, "I wish I were back in my mother's womb. I want to be with my own kind. I feel lonely. I would like to be out of this cage and run around." I could feel how much she needed her mother.

This bear showed me impressions of herself walking in the woods and just beginning to learn about the land and life forms around her. Now she was confused because she was no longer in the woods, and there was no one to teach her what she felt she needed to know to survive. The bear had an innate desire to learn these things, and so she experienced a void.

She started sucking her paw and crying. When I asked her why, she mentally showed me pictures of her mother and the woods, and I felt her sadness. This was no different than a child sucking a thumb for comfort.

Her caretaker planted trees in the pen to give her climbing exercise. I watched her learning about balance, coordination, and playing.

I could sense within this bear innate urges that wanted to come out, but she didn't know what to do with them within the confines of a pen.

After a while, she became more secure and began to make a transition from missing her mother to trusting humans. I was glad she was able to accept the change, but felt sad about her not having a life in the woods.

I knew her deep natural urges to be a bear, in a complete sense, could never be developed to their fullest potential. But on some level her soul had chosen to come into this circumstance.

Wise Gorilla

I HAVE BEEN COMMUNICATING telepathically for years with a delightful and colorful lowland gorilla. Barbara has given birth several times since I have known her. I tuned in to her experiences to see what it was like for her to be pregnant. Her pregnancies were difficult, and she suffered from problems familiar to women: discomfort, swollen ankles, tiredness.

Gorillas squat when giving birth, which is a natural and efficient position. Like humans, gorillas do not automatically know how to care for their newborns. They must be taught, and this gorilla had never been taught. All her babies were placed in the nursery because she did not know how to hold or nurse them. She communicated to me that she didn't know what to do with a newborn, but felt very upset when a baby was taken from her. Feelings of emptiness and sadness were conveyed to me when she said this about one of her newborns, "He's gone."

The feelings she experienced were not very different from those of a woman, simply expressed differently.

Fortunately, this particular gorilla bounced back fairly quickly because she was highly social and loved showing off for visitors. This gorilla was generally content living at the zoo except when she was pregnant or put in disruptive circumstances.

After being artificially inseminated, this same gorilla was removed from her grassy exhibit and placed into a small cage to try and avoid miscarriage. The building was dimly lit and she had no contact with her regular gorilla friends.

She communicated to me as she watched me through the black bars of her cage. Her communication was angry and passionate: "I want to be on grass, to run, express myself. Can't do that in here. Many think I have adjusted fine; not so. I don't know how long I can stand this. Things are not always what they seem, especially when it comes to one species viewing another. By being in here, there are limitations of sight, sound, and smell that your species hasn't yet begun to understand. Not sure you can. It is cruel to take me from where I was and put me in iron and concrete. I do feel, I hurt, love, and cry in my own ways. Just because there are no wet tears doesn't mean I don't have tears. This is not comprehended by humans.

"Tell me, do I look like I belong in this dark place? Of course not. I can be angry, though my Nature is gentle and peaceful. Do these actions seem normal? [nervous and repetitive actions with arms, hands and rest of body] They are not any more natural to me than to you. They develop for obvious and not so obvious reasons. It's difficult to entertain yourself the number of hours I am required to. I want to be with my kind. To touch, play, be on the grass and enjoy life again. Will I do that again?"

I communicated to her that she would be confined for a while, but that she would once again play with her friends on green grass. The time behind bars seemed like an eternity to her.

This wonderful gorilla teacher spoke to me further from her essence with great conviction, "I am more than a gorilla; I am you and you are me. How you treat me you treat yourselves. The respect and harmony that is meant to exist among all living beings is not being honored by humans. Those who have separated themselves from the meaning of mutual respect for all of life forget what relationships can be like. Humans try to stand alone and do not realize what they are creating for other life forms and the Earth. Long ago, loss of consciousness of natural ways led into unconscious activities and humans parted from Nature. What humans deem necessary in their course of evolution is not, and it is not what they think it is anyway.

"Humans, from their point of view, appear to be the most conscious animal. Not so. Humans seem to be the only ones who don't understand the scheme of things. Humans have been on an off-beaten track for so long, they can't hear the truth about harmonious connections and all the selfish choices that have caused other species to feel defeated.

"Open to the inner self. Will it ever be recognized we are all one? Other animals and beings have this awareness.

"The domestic animals have been trying for years to open up humans' eyes to their inner qualities, to not get lost in the outward form. This is part of the reason why the dog and cat have chosen to be humans' friends. There are close and great ties between species, but many humans fail to see them. Look into my eyes and beyond them. What do you see? Yourself, of course."

I sat in silence, and thanked her for her messages.

Animals in captivity can't actualize their potential the way they would in the wild. This is not to say all animals in zoos are horribly unhappy. In fact, a number of zoo animals are content. Yet they often remain shadows of their true selves. They have become something different from who they really are by being out of touch with their basic roots in Nature.

Animals born in captivity don't adjust innately to living in a zoo. The genetic memories from their ancestors are not forgotten or bred out.

Communicating with Animals in Zoos

THERE IS A DIFFERENCE between communicating telepathically with animals in zoos, animals in the wild, and domestic animals. When I telepathically reach out to zoo animals, I approach them more carefully and take more time than I typically do with domestic animals. Because they are wild animals, they sometimes guard themselves more, psychically, reacting more quickly than domestic animals, but not as fast as animals in the wild. Of course, it also depends on the individual animal. The majority of zoo animals are open to communicating and enjoy it, especially when someone takes a sincere interest in them. Then the animals can begin to trust that source of sincerity.

Kinship with a Chimpanzee

I HAD THE OPPORTUNITY to meet an adorable chimp a zookeeper friend of mine was raising for a zoo. Not only was she beautiful, but highly intelligent. She knew exactly how to wrap humans around her little chimp finger.

One of the first times we communicated, when she was six months old, she told me she missed her mother and had trouble adjusting to a humans' body texture. So my friend wore a furry vest.

I watched this chimp touch, taste, and handle everything she could get her hands on. From her spirit I heard, "I must be active and learning; that's how I would survive in the wild."

One day my zookeeper friend and I were sitting on the floor watching the chimp. I told her I was going to converse telepathically with the chimp for a few minutes. As the chimp and I established a heart-to-heart connection, she immediately stopped playing with her toys and stared at me while we communicated. My human friend couldn't believe it. The chimp's response was, "How can you communicate like this? It's not typical of humans I've encountered."

As the chimp began to grow, I had to fine-tune my intuitive abilities in order to flow with her incredibly quick mental pace. She was always mentally and physically a step or two ahead of me.

It was a gift to watch this chimp develop and grow physically, emotionally, intellectually, and spiritually. She taught me a great deal about myself and chimpanzees. One important lesson I learned was that if I sent thoughts her way while she was busy playing or if she just didn't want to converse, she would simply disregard them.

I had the privilege of visiting the chimp often, so we became good friends. At one point, she was becoming aware of peoples' noses, eyes, ears, and so on. She was noticing the similarities and differences between herself and humans. During this period she communicated, "I get confused and don't know who I am. But I am happy here." A little later she said silently, "I get lonely for my own species."

A few months later she expressed a fear of other chimps, yet part of her wanted to be with them.

One time I asked her about her dreams. She said that she dreamed of other chimps she had known before coming here. She also dreamed about her daily activities.

This chimp's imagination and creativity were endless. She was flexible, agile, fun, and intelligent. She reminded me how important it is to play in life. As I got to know her better, I had the opportunity to see her express all the same emotions we humans do, maybe not in exactly the same way, but I watched her express pain, love, sadness, joy, and other emotions.

Jacquelin and chimp communicating.

This chimp could communicate with ease. She could read my thoughts, feelings, and intentions like an open book. I had to be very centered when communicating with her. As is the case with other animals, she sees auras of other life forms.

One day, earlier in our relationship, I was jotting down notes about our time together. She grabbed my pen, stuck it in her mouth, and laughed out loud while scooting across the room. She knew I was easy to outsmart and that she could move faster than I. This playful chimp was teasing me with the pen and suddenly I heard, "Why are humans so slow? Why don't you watch and feel what I do instead of looking at the paper and writing?" She was right.

At tens months old, this ape's presence was overpowering at times—so strong, clever, agile, honest, graceful, kind, and mischievous, full of life and wonder.

One time, I had to wear an eye patch for a few days. When the chimp saw me, she hopped onto my lap, hugged me, and kissed the eye patch very gently. I was moved by her empathy. I could feel healing light moving into my eye. Her intuition was much more highly developed than that of humans. Her thoughts were like flashes of lightning and her body flowed like a melody in motion. She was creativity itself. From her spirit she channeled universal thoughts such as, "I am part of every soul, every being, and yet I am myself. I am spontaneity." This wonderful being had a number of chimp sitters, and I noticed how they all opened up whenever she was around.

It was great fun to watch this chimp play with her different dog friends. One day I introduced the chimp to a golden retriever. There was an instant rapport and understanding between these two species. They established ground rules for playing. Then they ran, rolled, twirled, and romped together for over an hour. It was a harmonious dance of two joyful spirits.

At one point during their play, a yellow butterfly caught the chimp's eye. She toddled after the butterfly and tried to touch it carefully with her hand. The look of delight, curiosity, and tenderness in this chimp's eyes expressed a boundless love of life as she discovered this wonderful winged creature.

As the dog and chimp were ending their playtime, the chimp reached out to embrace the golden retriever, but the dog backed away because of an outside interruption.

A genuine friendship quickly developed between the chimp and dog. Whenever I would drive over to visit the retriever's people, he would investigate my car looking for his friend, the chimp.

The relationship I had the privilege to take part in with this chimp, for over a year, touched me deeply.

Chapter Nine

Conversations With Wild Animals

In Africa, I had incredible opportunities to communicate with various forms of wildlife. One exciting, unforgettable experience was with an exquisite female baboon.

A small group of us were traveling in a van and stopped to click some photographs of a baboon troop. It was obvious that tourists passed through this particular area often, because the monkeys were not highly threatened. One person placed some crackers on the van's window sill. A number of females scampered up to the window, grabbed the goods, and made their getaway. Meanwhile, a frisky dominant male was continually trying to keep the females away from the van so he could partake in eating the crackers. As I sat and watched this great, fun game (for all of us), a female climbed to a point on the open roof of the van. There she sat, not more than two feet from my face, looking directly at me. I told her telepathically and verbally that she was the most beautiful creature I had ever seen. Along with this message I sent feelings of joy, openness, and admiration. She sat in a poised position upon the roof and stared with intent into my eyes. She had received my message and responded with an unbroken gaze. She let me know silently that she felt the friendly feelings and that they had surprised her.

"This is a different sensation than with other humans," she said. Most humans did not know how to open up and feel the heart-to-heart contact we were having.

We shared a special eye-to-eye connection until a couple of the van's occupants suddenly realized her presence on the roof. They became frightened and screamed, chasing the magnificent animal away with their fear. It felt as if a wonderful dream had suddenly been shattered. I was glad this wild creature and I had shared an experience of love and oneness.

I have never forgotten this experience. Years later, I wrote this poem about the encounter:

How It Was Before the Fall

Our guide stops the van, flips
the canvas rooftop open
so we can snap photos of a baboon
troop romping through umbrella trees.

I'm loading my Nikon with film
thud.
My eyes shoot up. A young baboon
with a doglike-muzzle is dancing
along the edges of the van's roof.

I set my camera down, sit still,
admire this girl. The woman next
to me screeches. Be quiet, I whisper.

Baboon hands wrap around the rim
of the open roof as she leans deep
into the van surveying us, wind
blowing her fur, tufted tail ticking the air.

I spot my reflection in her sun-filled
eyes. She looks through me.
Bone and flesh disappear,
aahhh, we are light to light.

Then we slip back into our bodies.
She gives me a sly smile
and glances back as she dashes off.

SINCE WILD ANIMALS live in Nature, their acute senses are more highly attuned to any disharmony in their environment. They must be constantly alert if they are to survive. This is a natural kind of sensory intelligence of the body, mind, and spirit.

At times, it is more of a challenge for wild animals to be open to communication with humans. This is partially because of our body scents, perfume, and clothing. This often is not a pleasant experience for the animals, since perfume and clothing are unnatural scents. Many of our systems are filled with polluted thoughts and foods. They smell and sense all that is within our systems—physically, mentally, emotionally, and spiritually. This can confuse and scare them.

Baboon gazing into Jacquelin's eyes.

As with domestic animals, some wild animals are more willing to communicate than others. Most young animals in the wild are open to communicating because they haven't yet learned to fear humans. But in time they learn to fear and "put off" the human animals. They learn that some of the two-leggeds carry weapons that can kill them from great distances.

When a wild animal is approached with an open, caring spirit, the animal is usually willing to communicate. Animals in the wild don't like to carry on long conversations because of their high level of sensitivity and continual concern for safety.

Some of them just want to move away from humans because they feel sickened by what they know this species is doing to them and the Earth. The animals communicate silently to each other about the destruction humans do to their homes and have done to their ancestors. They are confused as to why the human animal is this way.

Lions and cheetahs hunt and kill for food in order to live, but humans have an ongoing hunt to destroy and kill for no good reason.

Animals can feel poachers' intentions to kill them from afar and they pass this message on to their families as well as other animals. Some major disadvantages for animals in this situation can be their large bodies or the inability to escape from fast-moving vehicles or fast-traveling bullets. Others become confused, dawdle too long, or are just taken by surprise.

In America, wild animals like mountain lions have let me know they are fully aware of the damage humans are doing to their immediate habitats as well as the rest of the environment. They are sad and scared. Some species know their kind may vanish from the Earth forever.

ANIMALS RECEIVE mental, physical, and spiritual nourishment from the trees, grass, soil, and air. Life forms are one with the land. There is no separation. If the land is harmed, then the animals are harmed. If the animals are destroyed, the ecosystem is disrupted and eventually destroyed.

Butterflies cry in their own way as the air is deadened and darkened by pollution.

More and more humans on Earth are doing what they can to help animals and the environment. There is hope with all that is being done.

When wild animals are taken from their natural environment and put into unnatural surroundings, they lose that source of nurturing and balance, often becoming depressed, neurotic, or sick. This is what happens to many animals in zoos. Animals in the wild do not suffer from the neuroses and other problems that affect domestic animals.

If we watch wild animals, they can help reawaken our own primordial fountains. Animals living in Nature have a wisdom and knowledge we can relearn. They are our ancestors who carry unspoken, ancient stories in their hearts about the elements, about life, creation, and the Creator as well.

Wild Animals and Communication

SOME PEOPLE at my workshops mention that they are frightened to communicate with wild animals. They say they're afraid they might be overwhelmed by the animal's primal feelings. But these primal feelings are our ancestry, and can help us better understand why it's so important for us and them to remain connected with Nature.

Wild animals reflect the instinctual, free, wild, sensual side that our society rejects. We see ourselves in their eyes and hearts and in their dance with Nature. Only by feeling this within can we realize our wholeness and know our roots.

How We View Wild Animals

For thousands of years, we have told myths about wild animals, like King Kong, and so we still view some of them as dangerous to humans. Some animals are, but if we think they're dangerous, then danger is what we attract and encourage from them. If our intent is to kill them, then an animal becomes dangerous and rightly so.

Others see some wild animals as cute and cuddly stuffed bears, lions, or monkeys. This, too, is an unrealistic way to approach animals. When people do not understand or disregard body language that says, "stay away," and continue to move into an animal's personal space, the animal may attack as a last resort to protect herself or her young. For example, a lion's growl or an elephant's charge are clear messages. An attack is a result of our not listening to or respecting their warnings. Most animals would rather not attack. Animals often redirect and discharge their energy onto a bush or tree that's close at hand. This is a wonderful wisdom.

Here is an example of the way one person I watched disregarded an animal's signal. A woman walked past some tents we stayed in on the Serengeti plains and marched out into an area designated for animals only. She walked toward an elephant because she wanted to get some photographs. The elephant had warned the woman by first putting ears forward and getting into a charge position, but it was as though she was blind. The elephant started to charge. Some of the Masai men had to run out and distract the elephant so she wouldn't be injured.

Sometimes, animals are forced into defending themselves because we don't bother to learn or understand their language. Biologists Delia and Mark Owens have studied animals in the Kalahari desert. They became acquainted with a pride of lions who would saunter into their camp and stand at the foot of their bed. In their book, *Cry of the Kalahari*, they say, "As we learned to recognize facial expressions and postures that indicated their moods and intentions, and as they had become less curious about us, we found we had little to fear from them, as long as we did not create a setting that they might interpret as compromising or threatening. This is not to say that they had become house cats; we realized that they were still wild and potentially dangerous predators. Yet even when we blundered into them during the many times they had come into camp, they had never done us any harm."

Different species understand and respect each others' language very well. For example, zebras and lions drink from the same water hole side by side without incident. But if a hungry lioness is in the area, the zebras know it's not a safe time to drink.

Many wild animals in parks and reserves know that they are protected. There are instances of animals purposely traveling to game reserves in order to avoid being hunted.

It takes time and patience to be present with wild animals before they are ready to accept a human into their space. If someone feels fear or panic, they react accordingly. If one remains still and calm, the animal senses that and responds in kind.

Communicating with whales, fish, and other beings of the waters is done the same way as with other wild animals. This is because the heart-to-heart spiritual connection goes beyond any differences that we might perceive as barriers. Fish, whales, and most other water creatures need to be connected with in a gradual and gentle way, as with wild land animals. I have found the various beings to be open and friendly.

Africa

ONE WEEK I WAS LIVING in the midst of concrete, steel, plastic, power wires, noise, and sooty skies. The next week, I was living in wide open spaces of tall yellow grass, green trees, clear blue skies, and wild animals. It was so overwhelming to open fully and experience natural Nature that I had to close off a little at first to adjust.

I had the privilege of spending a week outside of game reserves hiking, or if I wanted to, riding a camel. (In parks and reserves you must remain in vans.) Our group hiked about ten miles a day.

My whole being could breathe here in ways that were difficult to experience back in Ohio. I expanded, danced, and moved in natural ways that felt intertwined with the acacia trees, mountains, grasses, rocks, soil, and animals. The telepathic communication the animals and I shared was enhanced by being in natural Nature. I felt totally connected to my ancient roots in Nature and in life. I felt I had come home.

Baboons

ONE AFTERNOON, a few of us were hiking around the base of a hill when we heard baboon vocalizations and barks coming from about the middle of the hill. We looked up and saw six baboons scampering around the brush and into trees. These baboons probably had never seen humans. I was so excited at first, I couldn't stay still inside long enough to communicate with them. Then I centered myself and began to send out friendly feelings in their direction. I heard, "What are you doing here, who are you?" They felt threatened by us strange animals, and wanted us to stop looking at them. Then a few of the baboons ran down the hill, barked, and hurried back into some straggly bushes. I did not look directly at them; I communicated that we would not approach or harm them in any way and that we were animals who appreciated them. I asked if anyone was willing to communicate with me for a few minutes. I ran into their walls of suspicion and backed off. After some time passed and they had traveled farther up the hill, they felt safer and were more open about communicating.

Game Reserves

IT WAS THRILLING TO SEE wild animals in their natural environment. Through observation and nonverbal communication, I experienced the differences between these animals I met in the wild and those of the same species in game parks. Even more significant were the differences between animals in the wild and those residing in zoos.

I especially noticed this when we left the wild areas and traveled to a game reserve where people go out in vans to view the animals.

The first day there, after getting settled in my tent, I walked out to find zebras, baboons, and elephants walking around in an area where animals can be viewed by tourists. It was a dramatic change from the animals I had glimpsed outside the reserve. The animals here would come and go, knowing they were safe, and seemed to tolerate the humans living in this area. Of course, they could always leave.

One baboon scooted up and sat within four feet of me. He was curious about my camera and notepad. I sent out friendly feelings, and he responded with openness. I was careful not to physically intrude into his space.

Silently, I asked him what he felt about this area where humans stared, took pictures, and talked to him. This handsome baboon's response was, "This is fun and usually I feel happy coming into contact with humans. I don't like the ones who shout, point fingers, or attempt to chase me. They make me nervous. But I can take care of myself, so I'm not usually afraid. I have been coming here for several years. Other baboons showed me this place, told me it was safe and that humans wouldn't bother us. It's fun to watch humans' funny actions and see the strange objects (cameras, etc.) they carry or lay on the ground. I like to try to take some of those objects when humans aren't looking."

It was a delightful conversation and we had several exchanges during my stay at this camp.

An elephant told me, "I know it's safe here and we won't be touched, but these humans can get pesky. I had to gradually become used to humans."

Serengeti Plains

VENTURING OUT IN A VAN to see animals was fun. On the first run, I saw three cheetahs and several rhinoceros. The cheetahs were elegant, graceful beings who tolerated our presence. And the sturdy rhinos stood and looked at us as if to say, "You came all the way out here on the plains to watch us graze?"

I had expected these animals to exit as we approached, but they just remained where they were. They knew humans generally wouldn't harm them here. I was thrilled to see them only yards in front of me, yet felt conflicted because we humans were constantly invading their territory.

One experience I shall never forget was watching a wildebeest being born. Our van stayed a good distance away as we watched through camera lenses so as not to disturb them. The newborn fell to the Earth within one minute. She was steady on her legs and running alongside her mother with the rest of the herd within ten minutes.

I let my energy flow gently toward the mother and calf a little while after this birthing. I wanted to sense their feelings. I felt the calf's tremendous inborn physical and spiritual drive to move, get up, and run as soon as she saw light and breathed the Earth's air. The mother's innate urge was to get her newborn up on all fours and running before she'd allow her calf to nurse. The wildebeest is an animal of prey. It was great to feel their primal energies.

Crowned Cranes

ONE DAY I WAS OUTSIDE alone sunning myself while staying at a lodge in Rwanda. A male and female crowned crane slowly began to ease toward me. They carried themselves gracefully, like moving sculptures. I let them know I would remain still and invited them to come closer for a visit. After a short time, they paraded less than a foot in front of me in gowns of white feathers and multi-colored crowns. One of them pecked on my knee and foot and then stood next to me. All three of us made heart-to-heart connections. Joy and appreciation streamed from my heart to both of them. They communicated, "We are a little apprehensive but friendly. We know we are safe in this area and would like to know more about humans. We have seen humans but haven't had any of them communicate with us in this way."

They wanted to know why we were there, what we were looking for, who were our enemies and allies. I explained that I was here to experience the beauty of Africa and her creatures. We exchanged thoughts until the evening sun melted into the land.

Mountain Gorillas

THERE ARE ABOUT three hundred mountain gorillas left in Rwanda. Rwanda, in central Africa, is one of the smallest and poorest African countries. It has the highest human density, with about five million people living in an area the size of Maryland. The gorillas live in the Virunga Volcanoes in the Rwandan Volcanoes National Park.

If it wasn't for the anti-poaching efforts of the late naturalist Diane Fossey and other concerned individuals to save their habitat, the gorillas would now be extinct. Yet they are still threatened by poaching, human encroachment on their land, and war. Half of their habitat has been turned into fields for planting crops. The war has destroyed much of the land.

Wire snares (usually set to catch smaller animals), guns, and spears have been used to poach gorillas for hands, heads, and feet which are sold as costly souvenirs. Baby gorillas are captured to sell as pets, mainly to Europeans.

The Mountain Gorilla Project, a government project, has habituated some gorilla groups so that small clusters of tourists can see them, while the park earns money and generates revenue. Another purpose of the project is to educate the Rwandese about the gorillas and their plight.

As we entered the park early in the morning, we were given walking sticks and a lunch. We were introduced to two guides who would lead us into the habitat of a group of mountain gorillas. They informed us that we would be seeing a group that was just becoming habituated to people. Rwanda is at about 7,500 feet above sea level, and we were going to continue climbing up the side of a volcano, Visoke, to about twelve thousand feet.

As our small group began to slowly move up this steep mountain, it was like entering a magical land. The rich, thick vegetation was unbelievably beautiful. The volcanoes were wrapped in morning mist and their peaks gazed down on me. Venturing further into this lush land, I could see and feel the extremely dense green herbage and tree canopies. They were magnificent. Long, thick, full vines and growth were above, below, and all around me, forming walls of solid green. While making my way through the forest, a number of times I would take a step and suddenly sink knee-deep in soft mud and get stuck. Dozens of vines were wrapped around my shoes and hugging my thighs. The others would grab my arms and yank me up and out.

After almost three hours of fast slipping and sliding through mud, nettles, trees, and vines, the guide spotted the gorillas' nest, which had dung in it from the previous night.

He knew exactly where to go and we followed. At this point I was right behind him. The guide uttered friendly gorilla vocalizations to the gorillas. We saw bushes begin to move. Suddenly, the guide pulled my body beside his. Right before my eyes a silverback, the leader of the group, was sitting on a pile of vines, munching away on stalks of wild celery. He was about fifteen feet away and was keenly aware of our presence. The guide said the gorilla's name was Chief. Chief rose out of the shadows and moved toward us. He explored us with his eyes. Since most of us had been around gorillas, we knew to crouch and look down in order to show submission and respect.

I sent Chief sincere feelings of admiration and respect. I never felt fearful because I know gorillas are peaceful creatures if no one bothers them. Only if humans are aggressive and the gorillas feel cornered would they attack.

The vegetation was so dense, most times I could see only five to fifteen feet in front of me. As we continued to creep along, I saw two young male juveniles whirling through leafage. Then I turned to catch a quick glimpse of two older juveniles scurrying out of sight in the foliage. (These two were missing hands because snare traps had cut them off.) The younger juveniles were concentrating on chewing wild celery and didn't seem bothered by our presence. One juvenile scooted by about four feet in front of me, tossed himself through some leaves, and began playing among bamboo.

I telepathically asked one of the juveniles how he felt about our being here and he silently said, "I feel comfortable as long as you don't encroach on my space or body."

The silverback communicated saying, "I am a little nervous and concerned. I smell humans' presence at times even though I don't see many of them. Do you want something? Don't try to take anyone away; this is our family."

It was easy to see why he had these concerns and questions, especially since his group was in the early stages of being habituated to humans and had probably encountered poachers.

When I went beyond his personality and communed with his spirit, I heard, "I see, hear, and know the other forms' beingness in the jungle, as they know mine. This is living with the jungle. We are each other."

We spent only about a half-hour with them, since they weren't accustomed to humans being so close. But it was incredible to get to spend time with them.

My reactions to being with the gorillas were different from what I had anticipated. I expected to be ecstatic, and wondered if I could contain myself. I experienced great joy, but also felt somewhat uncomfortable intruding their territory.

Tourists' dollars can help save the gorillas and their habitat, but humans could still destroy them because they disrupt their natural ways of living. I don't know if there are any perfect solutions for the gorillas or for most of the other animals and life forms, including humans, who are caught in similar circumstances.

Through this experience I was able to have a tiny glance into Dian Fossey's world, and the never-ending struggle to protect the gorillas from poachers, farmers, and war. I had the privilege to meet and talk with Dian Fossey at a lecture before she was savagely murdered in 1985. I asked her if she felt the gorillas communicated nonverbally with her and she said, "Of course." Most people thought that one day she would be killed by gorillas. The irony is that she was brutally attacked and murdered by her own kind.

All the wild animals are treasures of the Earth. Let us care for them with gentleness, respect, and love.

Chapter Ten

Understanding and Supporting the Animals We Love

ANIMAL COMPANIONS offer humans many incredible gifts, and it's a privilege to live with them. They accept and love us unconditionally. Animals forgive us for stepping on their tails and paws, or for yelling at them after a bad day at work. They tolerate our lifestyles. Animals, by Nature, remind us there's more to life than our careers and problems.

Animals literally change peoples' lives because of who they are and what they give. Animals help those in nursing homes, hospitals, prisons, and other institutions. Animal companions alleviate loneliness, and when petted, lower people's blood pressure. Heart attack victims live longer when residing with an animal friend. Animals help to make breakthroughs with depressed and autistic people. Animals residing in penal institutions help reduce hostility among prisoners. Overall, statistics show that people who have an animal companion live longer.

Teachers and Healers

ANIMALS HEAL US by fulfilling many mental, emotional, spiritual, and physical needs. Our life-giving friends teach us how to trust and open up. They encourage us to allow our best qualities to emerge.

Chloe and Etheria helped teach people about telepathic communication at my workshops. They were clear, strong communicators, and could be humorous, too. They were able to transform some peoples' closed attitudes about cats and birds.

Etheria would spread her wings and strut around the floor talking telepathically to everyone.

Chloe, Etheria, and I also journeyed into other realms astrally to work with angels and beings of light for healing of others as well as ourselves.

ONE OF THE MOST GIFTED healers I have ever met was a golden retriever named Ted. He was a born healer, a highly evolved soul. Rooms would light up and be filled with love when he bounced in. Everywhere he went people were drawn to him. Ted healed people by radiating light. That light would touch and heal people in whatever ways they might need, even if they weren't aware of what they needed.

Ted died of cancer (he took on too many peoples' energies—not all of them willingly), but communicated to me he was ready to move on because his purpose had been fulfilled in helping others (especially his person, Karen, and dog sister, Betty) to heal.

Just before Ted died, there was a long procession of people who thanked him and said goodbye.

Interaction

FROM AN INTUITIVE LEVEL, I have watched people and animals interact in physical, emotional, spiritual, and mental ways. I use my inner eyes and senses to perceive the exchanges of energies. Because animals are so connected to the Earth they automatically help to center and ground people. This is one reason why animals are highly successful healers and therapists.

I saw peoples' energy fields go through significant changes while I watched them pet goats at a children's zoo one day. As the people approached the animals, their energy fields expanded outward like a light bulb being turned on. They were opening to the animal. When adults were apprehensive about approaching an animal, their energy fields wavered, or constricted. After a while, if a person felt comfortable with an animal, their energy field expanded, but not to the extent of those who really wanted to be with the animal. I noticed that young children had the most dramatic shooting outward of energy fields.

Animals are positive for us because they ignite that spark of spontaneity, our inner child aspect, that we often forget to nourish.

One day, I was walking with a very reserved man around the zoo. As soon as we stood in front of the tigers' exhibit, he suddenly started darting back and forth in perfect timing with the tigers. I stood in amazement at his instant transformation from reserved adult to exuberant child.

Animal Needs

LET US REMEMBER to appreciate all the animals who touch our lives. Let's look at some needs animals have and how we can fill them.

Our animal companions have mental, emotional, physical, and spiritual needs. They are social beings who want to actualize their Nature and fulfill their purpose, as we do.

This example shows how easy it is to misunderstand an animal's needs. One woman works from nine until nine almost every day of the week. Her two dogs are in the yard all this time. She lets them in the house, now and then, before going to bed. These dogs told me they felt they had no purpose and were very depressed. Even though they had one another for companionship, it was still obvious they were starving for attention from their human.

Let us remember that animal friends need more than food, water, a pat on the head, or an evening walk. When needs aren't met, misbehaviors or illness can be the result.

It's important to understand the traits or purpose of each breed. For example, a German shepherd was bred to herd sheep but is very efficient in watching over children. It would be good for people to consider what breed complements their personality and lifestyle when choosing a dog or cat companion.

Animals are creative, intelligent beings and if we encourage this and other natural qualities, we will truly see the animals become themselves. Let them express their animal Nature. Respect the individuality of each animal and learn how they communicate. Allow an animal to expand and mature.

Animals tell me they feel dishonored if we are overprotective and talk down to them in baby talk. Encourage your animal companions to be who they are and to live up to their fullest potentials.

Leave Me Alone

DO WE PAY ATTENTION when our animals tell us, in a variety of ways, when they want to be left alone? We need to be sensitive to the way they respond to our touch so as to respect their boundaries. It's not appropriate to force ourselves on animals, not listening to the fact that the animal is struggling to get away. Animals need psychological and physical space from others as we do; this is especially true with an animal who lives indoors. But animals also need our companionship since many of them are alone all day. It's a matter of listening telepathically to the animal and observing her body language.

One time I walked up to a pony and started brushing his mane. He swung his head around and silently said, "Why don't you introduce yourself before you start brushing me?" I felt embarrassed and started again by introducing myself. I realized how I had just sauntered into his space and started touching him without asking if it was okay. I wouldn't do that with a person, so why did I assume it was fine to approach him in this way? I have never forgotten that important lesson.

Children and Animals

YOUNG CHILDREN AND ANIMALS can communicate telepathically in a natural way. This is because a child hasn't yet been taught to disregard intuition. But it is important to teach a child how to respect an animal's physical body, feelings, and other needs. When an animal and young child play together, an adult should be present to oversee the situation. This way, the boundaries of both species are considered and the animal and child don't unknowingly hurt each other. An animal usually senses what appropriate boundaries are with a child. Overstepping boundaries can happen if the child grabs the animal's body or if the animal overwhelms the child through overzealous play. Both child and animal need to feel they are in a secure environment.

It can be difficult for an animal when a child is born. Sometimes an animal may become jealous, so we should nonverbally show and tell her about the changes. This way she knows that she's not being replaced or pushed aside. When a baby is born, the animal needs as much and probably more affection to be reassured that she's loved and wanted. It can also be communicated to the animal how they can take part in caring for this new creature in the home.

I often suggest that before a baby is born the family members carry a doll around so the animal can adjust to the idea of another being entering the family.

Healing with Your Hands

WHEN SOMEONE CALLS ME for a consultation, one of the first questions I ask them is if their animal companion has been examined by a veterinarian. If not, I ask them to do so. The techniques mentioned in this chapter are to be used as complementary to veterinary medicine and are not intended to replace it. I do not diagnose or treat diseases, but I may offer information I receive from an animal for the person to share with their veterinarian.

There are various ways we can help awaken the natural healing properties that flow within our animal companions.

Using your hands in a healing manner can help misplaced or blocked energy to discharge and helps to align the body's systems. I call this technique "Healing With Hands." Simply hold your hands about three inches above an animal and slowly move your hands over the animal, imaging healing light moving out through your hands and into the animal. It's important to begin at the head and move towards the tail, from the top of the back, down the legs and to the paws. This follows the natural flow of the body's systems. Some people sense or feel the blocked or flowing energy but this is not necessary in order for this technique to work. It's the life force within that knows how to heal the animal.

It doesn't take much healing energy to help an animal, so I often recommend doing the work within the animal's energy fields rather than actually touching them.

Too Much Energy

A NUMBER OF ANIMALS have communicated to me that their people are sending too much energy into their bodies and energy fields. This can create imbalances and can cause problems in the flow of Kundalini energy, which rises naturally from the base of the spine upward through the chakra system. More animals are asking me to tell their person to do a lot less energy work because it doesn't take much to awaken their own healing system.

One woman called me and said she was doing energy work on her cat four times a week trying to work out a "tic" in the cat's neck. The cat shouted at me, "Tell her to stop. The energy is so much that now I have a tic in my neck." The woman did not realize that she was burning her cat out with too much energy and that the overabundance of energy had created the tic.

LYNDA AND HER DOG COMPANION Holly have a very close bond. When Lynda first started her training in Reiki, she would try and treat Holly by placing her hands directly on Holly. Holly is extremely sensitive to energy and the Reiki was too much for her. Lynda soon learned that she could place her hands about six inches above Holly's body with positive results.

One time, Lynda noticed that if her stomach bothered her during the night, Holly's stomach would also start gurgling and then Holly would become ill by morning. Lynda realized Holly was absorbing her own energy during sleep. (Holly sleeps against Lynda.)

One night Lynda's stomach started giving her trouble. She also heard Holly's stomach making noises. Lynda started to do Reiki on herself, and within sixty seconds, Holly's stomach got quiet. Lynda was amazed and excited.

Now, when Holly's stomach makes noises during the night, Lynda knows she's the cause. She pulls the energy that Holly has absorbed from her back to herself. Then she performs Reiki on herself and within minutes, Holly's stomach returns to normal.

Angels

IN ALL THE WORK I do with animals, I always ask for the angels of light, including Archangel Raphael, whose name means "God has healed" to heal the animals in whatever way is best for them. As they do their work, I hear them sing their beautiful, unearthly songs and watch as they weave neon rainbows through an animal's energetic and physical bodies.

I was doing long-distance healing work with a dog, Joey, and I asked the angels to help heal his spinal column. The prognosis wasn't good. Joey had trouble standing and one hind leg was not functioning much. But after the angels spent time with Joey, administering their healing love and light, he started to move the leg more easily.

The angels and I, you could say, work as a team when I do healing and Soul Recovery work (see chapter 12).

Tellington TTouch

A GREAT WAY TO IMPROVE overall health and help facilitate behavioral change is Tellington TTouch, created by Linda Tellington-Jones. I had the opportunity to learn the TTouch from Linda at a workshop in 1986 and have used it on hundreds of animals through the years.

Linda describes the technique this way, in her book *The Tellington TTouch.*"You make circles holding your fingertips, your fingers, or your hand in various positions using varying pressures.

"The circles of the TTouch seem to provide a way for this 'cellular intelligence' common to all life to become communication, for the cells of one being to make a direct connection with the cells of another.

"Your circular motion wakes up the cells of that other being, activating them to let go of pain, 'dis-ease' or the expectation of pain, and allowing them to 're-member' their encoded potential for perfection."

The techniques described in this book can be used with any species.

ONE DAY, ANN CALLED and said her dog Sunrise had fallen off a cliff and that she had rushed her to a veterinary clinic. Sunrise had broken and fractured bones in the pelvic area. The veterinarians thought the sciatic nerve had been severed and that they might have to amputate her right hind leg.

The next morning I did the TTouch with wonderful results. Sunrise started to breathe deeply, which told me she was letting go of anxiety and relaxing her body. She stretched her body and took even deeper breaths and let go of some of the emotional and physical trauma. We watched Sunrise transform into a more relaxed dog. Ann said it was the first time since Sunrise had been at the hospital that she had seen her stretch, breathe normally, and let go of some of the pain.

I did TTouch to help Sunrise strengthen her body before surgery. This way of touching begins an immediate healing process within the cells.

Sunrise's surgery went well, and the sciatic nerve was intact so they did not have to amputate her leg. Ann and I did the TTouch and started using it with Sunrise after her surgery.

We worked with Sunrise on a regular basis for six weeks and felt that the TTouch, along with the use of Bach Flower Remedies, color therapy, crystal therapy, and other methods, helped Sunrise to recover more quickly and more completely. I also mentally talked to the cells within her body and asked them to reorganize themselves to accept, work with, and heal around the metal plate now in her thigh. (Every cell has an intelligence and responds to genuine concern and good feelings sent their way.) I also did circles around the head area, which helped her to release the emotional trauma from the fall. Sunrise is doing very well and has almost full use of her once badly damaged leg.

MISSEY, AN ADORABLE mixed breed, was at times limping around the house. She was under a veterinarian's care for arthritis. She asked me to use the TTouch, even though Missey's person, Gloria, told me she wouldn't let anyone touch her ears, legs, or tail without snapping. I approached her gently and slowly. I started doing circles on Missey's ears and on her body.

When I telepathically asked Missey about her pains, she showed me images of a man who was fearful of getting older. She communicated that she was absorbing his aches and pains. When I mentioned this to Gloria, she laughed and said, "Both my mother and I noticed that Missey limps more and seems older when Dad hobbles around complaining about aches and pains." His behavior reinforced Missey's own aches and pains. By the time the session was finished, she was totally relaxed and I could touch her anywhere on her body without any protest. Gloria later said that Missey was running around like a puppy again.

ANOTHER DOG, TOOTSIE, had been backed over while lying under the wheel of her person's car. There were no broken bones, but there was a lot of bruising and she couldn't walk. In conjunction with veterinary care, I used Healing With Hands, the TTouch, crystals, and Bach Flower Remedies. By the next morning she was starting to stand and walk around.

Any kind of touching is a matter of being with and being sensitive to the animal rather than "doing something to" the animal.

Quick or nervous petting and patting or an overly firm touch stimulates the body, making an animal feel nervous. Stroking an animal's fur in the opposite direction from which it lies stimulates and irritates. By initiating physical contact slowly and stroking with a firm yet gentle, open, flowing loving hand, you create relaxation and enhance health.

Skin Ailments

AN ANIMAL'S PHYSICAL state often reflects their mental and emotional state. Some problems that appear to be purely physical can stem from emotional issues. But pollution, diet, and other factors also contribute to problems.

ONE CAT, AMANDA, was diagnosed by a veterinarian as having psychogenic alopecia. This meant the origin of her problem, hair falling out in patches, was emotional rather than physical. Her condition had been going on for a few years, and nothing seemed to help for long.

Amanda silently told me she was very nervous partly because her person had moved a number of times, and she didn't like it. Also, that her person was highly nervous and that she absorbed and acted out this nervousness. I then saw an image in my mind of Amanda knotted up in a tight ball.

I suggested to the feline's person Celia that she relax, play, and have fun with Amanda, and that she play soothing music and visualize Amanda with thick brown fur. Amanda's fur grew back completely and stayed that way for months. She was doing fine until Celia had to deal with a hospitalized father and sick uncle. Then Amanda's fur started to fall out again.

A DOG NAMED THOMAS had a severe skin problem. His skin was red where patches of hair had fallen out. A veterinarian had treated him with antibiotics but there was no improvement.

I talked with Thomas and he communicated that his person John was nervous and always busy. The man told me his mother had died during the past year and he was still coping with his loss. As a result, he had become more nervous and Thomas absorbed his feelings.

I suggested that John play soft classical music for Thomas when he was away from home, and that he place his hands above him and imagine golden light flowing into him. John and I also discussed Thomas being put on a better diet.

The insights into this situation helped John to better understand himself and Thomas, which helped heal both of them. Within a month Thomas's skin and hair were normal and healthy.

Noise

MANY ANIMALS COMMUNICATE that noise is a problem for them because of their acute sensitivity to sound. Sounds are vibrational waves that travel through our bodies, greatly affecting animals and us.

One dog was snapping at people because her person played a stereo so loud that it was hurting the dog's body, making her nervous, irritable, and reactive. When the woman turned her stereo down the dog stopped snapping.

There is a great deal of noise pollution in our society, so we must be aware of how to protect our animals as much as possible. If an animal isn't used to loud sounds and is suddenly thrust into a noisy place, her behavior may change or she may become ill. If I cannot remove an animal from a noisy situation, I place them in a bubble of green light to help calm down their nervous system. I also ask the animal and her guardian angels to try to shut out the intensity of the noise.

Names

NAMES THAT WE GIVE animal companions are significant because they are vibrations of energy. Sometimes an animal may not like the vibration of their name. Animals do respond to their names and understand some words, but what they feel is the emotional tone of the person saying the name and the sound of the name. This is why it's important for a person to choose a name that brings up positive feelings for them. One cocker spaniel, Booboo, told me he greatly disliked the sound of his name and wished his people would change it. A cat told me she didn't like being called "baby" because of the way her person said it.

If we call an animal "beautiful and wise" this brings out their best qualities. If we refer to them as a "dummy" or "killer," then that is what we encourage because of our emotional energy that is present when we use words. A name should have uplifting feelings for the person and animal companion.

Birth Trauma

AFTER COMMUNICATING with animals for a while, I discovered that a number of them mentioned how traumatic birth had been for them. Problems can result from birth experience. At times, the birth experience can create crimps in the energy bodies and can even cause energy bodies to dissociate, which affects emotions and behavior. This is also true of humans.

A KITTEN, ANNA, said, "I had a very difficult time coming into this world. I couldn't breathe and was scared. Everything was moving around. My shoulder and neck hurt. So much pressure on my body. The kinks aren't out of my system yet. I was torn from my mother and it was painful. My whole world changed in an instant. One minute she's there, the next she's not. Someone with big hands took me away from her."

I do Soul Recovery with animals who have had difficult births or other major traumas. I find that this often heals them quickly and in a lasting way. In Soul Recovery work I gather all the dissociated parts of the animal and gently put them back into their proper place and align all energetic systems. Through this work, the animal regains their wholeness and can live life in a fuller way.

Early Issues

MANY KITTENS ALSO bring up their struggles during early kittenhood. Toby, the cat I discussed in chapter 7, talked about being born under porch steps and snuggling next to his mother for warmth during cold weather. He struggled to stay alive. While still very young, he was taken from his mother and given to a young girl. Toby said he hated being taken and felt sick because he missed his mother. Toby has trouble trusting humans and part of that is due to having been taken away from his mother at such a young age.

Letting animals like Anna and Toby show me what they have been through allows them to discharge the emotional pain.

Most of us don't stop to think of the effects of suddenly taking a young kitten or puppy away from their mother and placing them in a home. This can take away their sense of security, which can result in later problems. Ideally, a kitten or puppy should remain with their mother until they're at least twelve weeks old.

Mother animals naturally handle, touch, and clean their young. If humans touch and handle them during the first five weeks of life, they adjust well to us. Also, they are generally more adaptive than those not handled while quite young.

One way to help a very young animal who has been separated from her mother is to cradle her body against your heart area. Hearing a heartbeat has a quieting effect and offers a sense of inner security. Of course, you need to be relaxed before doing this. There are also soft cushions you can buy that contain a program of the heart beating.

Bach Flowers, Healing With Your Hands, and TTouch can also be helpful.

Helpful Healing Alternatives

Bach Flower Remedies are used to help shift emotional problems. They primarily work with the emotions, attitudes and energy of the animal. They are dilute infusions of flowers and tree buds. Bach Flowers work quickly with animals, and are advantageous to use for dealing with behavioral issues. There are many good books available on using Bach Flowers with animals.

Crystals have been used for hundreds of years for healing. It has been shown through Kirlian photography how within a short amount of time, a crystal strengthens the overall electromagnetic field, or energy, of an animal. Placing a crystal in the environment of a sick animal can assist healing. I placed a crystal into a fishbowl to help a sick fish, and within a few days he completely recovered. Crystals can help animals with various problems, but because of the high amount of energy they emit, they must be used with knowledge. There is a wide variety of good books on how to use crystals.

Color Therapy encourages balance and healing within the body. Various colors can be visualized as moving through the body to achieve specific states or help heal. Green can be used to balance, while golden light enhances overall health. If an animal is ill, you may have them lie on a gold or green colored rug, or perhaps put a green light bulb into a lamp in a room they are sleeping in. But read about color therapy before you decide to try it.

Massage is an excellent way of relaxing and offering healing energy to the body. I suggest reading *The Healing Touch* by Dr. Michael W. Fox.

Visualization is another useful technique. You can visualize the animal having exactly what he needs. If he is not feeling well, image him in perfect health. The cells will get this message and it will encourage healing. If he is hyper, visualize him being calm. Visualization can also be used while doing touch techniques. Remember, thought is energy, so visualization is powerful.

Telepathic communication enables us to be tuned in to our animals' feelings and needs. One day Chloe communicated to me—even though she wasn't acting any differently—that the right side of her mouth was hurting. I took her into the veterinarian who cleaned her teeth. After he was through, he said there was a problem with one of her molars on the right side. I'm glad she had communicated this to me.

Long Distance Healing. If an animal is not in your presence and you wish to send her healing energy, send the energy in the same way you would during telepathic communication. Having a photo of the animal may make it easier for you to visualize and send the energy-filled images. Make the initial heart-to-heart connection and let healing energy flow to the animal and see her in perfect health.

Affirmation Tapes

I DISCOVERED WHILE LEADING people through meditations that my animals were also responding accordingly to my words and intentions. I decided to record some cassette tapes for them. They work. I encourage people to make affirmation tapes for their animals. You can also make tapes to help an animal shed misbehaviors or to help them deal with a change of routine.

Before I go on a vacation, I make a tape that tells my animal companions I love them, that everything is fine, that they are safe, and to have fun. I also tell them that I will be coming home soon. Whoever is staying with my animals plays the tape once or twice a day. Quiet background music can be a great addition to a tape. Etheria, my cockatiel companion, loved violin music, while Chloe enjoyed the sound of bells, flutes, and trickling streams.

Love Heals

LOVE IS A POWERFUL BASIS from which to help an animal friend heal. One cocker spaniel, Sashi, was paralyzed in the hindquarters for months. A husband and wife were told by their veterinarian that their dog would not get better and suggested they have her euthanized. Sashi's people deeply loved her and decided to work with her. The man built a special cart so Sashi could get around. (Her front legs pulled the cart.) After several months sensation was returning in her legs and she was beginning to walk. They had been encouraging her emotionally and caring for her physical needs, along with giving their boundless love and patience. Within a couple more months she was walking almost normally. The veterinarian's response was, "It's a miracle."

HOLISTIC ALTERNATIVES can be used in conjunction with, and can greatly enhance traditional treatment. Once again, alternative ways are not intended to replace medical treatment but are to be used in conjunction with veterinary medicine.

Supporting Animals' Needs: Let us be sensitive to and allow animals to experience their feelings, whether it be joy, sadness, love, or grief. This helps an animal to discharge pent-up energies. The more aware we are of our own feelings, the more we can be aware of their feelings and needs.

Play: The importance of play to our animals and us cannot be overstated. Play keeps us young, open, spontaneous, and healthy. Animals are masters at play and teach us how to be in tune with ourselves, others, and them. Play allows our intuition to blossom like a flower and flow like a river.

Household Safety: One animal had this to say about our environment: "There are substances in the air that are affecting animals in physical, mental, and emotional ways. This wears our systems down until they are more open to taking in pollutants and the imbalanced vibrations of humans. I hope humans learn how to nurture and harmonize with themselves, others, and the Earth."

Today, in animals and people, we are seeing the results of the chemicals that we have spread over the Earth and through the atmosphere. We seldom think of the conglomeration of chemicals in our households that greatly contribute to polluting our living space and the air we breathe every day.

One woman's dog companion died due to chemicals. I asked the woman if there were any sprays, poisons, or plants in her home that the dog could have gotten ahold of. Her response was, "Well, people spray the house for roaches and other people spray the yard."

When I asked her dog who was in the light for insight concerning her death, she said, "The fumes from the spraying were slowly absorbed and accumulated in my system. Couldn't get away from them."

One afternoon I came home and found Chloe acting strangely. She told me someone had been there. I smelled spray and discovered that my landlord had had my home sprayed without my knowledge. Chloe acted subdued and ate very little for three days as a result of the spray. She said, "I feel sick to my stomach."

The spray made me feel sick; think what an animal with a smaller body and a highly developed sense of smell feels.

Many animals die every year from pesticides and other chemicals released into our environment. Today, there is a wide variety of natural housecleaning agents on the market to choose from. No one can make their home one hundred percent safe, but think about what objects in the home could be dangerous to an animal and put them out of reach.

One woman I know rushed her Siamese cat to the veterinarian because he was panting and salivating. The veterinarian opened the cat's mouth and found several sewing needles embedded deep in the throat. They had to be surgically removed.

Let us become more aware of how to protect our animal companions whom we love so deeply.

Body, Mind, and Spirit

People are becoming aware of how their lifestyles and diets affect themselves as well as their animal friends. More veterinarians are treating the whole animal rather than just the body. Mind, body, and spirit cannot be separated in dealing with health and behavior issues.

Acupressure, acupuncture, crystals, magnetic therapy, Bach Flowers, homeopathic remedies, herbs, vitamin and mineral supplements, and a healthy diet are some ways we can use to assist animals. These and others can support and strengthen an animal's immune system and overall health.

Working holistically is a natural way to help the whole being restore inner order and harmony. Sunshine, exercise, fresh air, good food, and good water greatly enhance general health. There are many books available that give information on holistic alternatives, so check them out.

Since we are responsible for the welfare of our animal companions, let us do what we can to enhance their lives.

Some questions you might want to ask yourself to see if your animal friend's needs are being met are:

1. Do I spend enough time with them and do I give them my full attention?
2. Do I telepathically and verbally talk with them often enough?
3. Are they included in my daily activities? Do I give them enough play and exercise?
4. Do I feed them good quality food?
5. Do I show them plenty of love and affection?

If your animal companion is misbehaving, these are basic questions to ask yourself. Perhaps some need is not being met and the animal is letting you know.

There are many ways to be supportive with our animals. Animals give us the gift of themselves. Let us give what we can to enhance their overall health of body, mind, emotions, spirit, and soul.

Chapter Eleven

Locating Lost Animals

LOCATING LOST ANIMALS is probably the most challenging work any animal communicator does. I have been tracking lost animals for over twenty years with good results.

I wrote the following story, which was published by *Cat Fancy Magazine* in 1984. This earlier experience encouraged me to continue to help people find their lost animal companions.

The Lost Feline

IT WAS EARLY MORNING when the phone rang. On the other end of the phone was a hysterical woman, Susie. "It's my cat, T.C. He's gone! Can you help me? He's been gone all night and has never been outside before," she cried.

I knew from personal experience the feeling of panic that fills a person when their animal friend disappears.

I asked her for a physical description of T.C., and if she knew when he had escaped from the house. Susie described him as a sleek, black cat with brilliant yellow eyes. She had discovered him missing the evening before and had no idea how he had gotten out of the house. I told her I would do my best to locate T.C. We hung up the phone. I sat down, took a deep breath, and set my intention to find him. I called his name silently. This allowed me, on a telepathic level, to reach out and establish a clear connection with the runaway.

Immediately, I sensed that he was scared out of his whiskers. After this initial contact, I was able to look through his eyes. As I looked around, I saw, directly behind him, a white wooden house with something yellow near the door. I felt him pressed against the house's foundation—huddled on cracked cement behind some bushes. I perceived that he was somewhere near Susie's house, but too petrified to respond to his name.

As I continued to listen telepathically, a confusing image emerged. I saw him several streets in back of Susie's residence. How could he be in two places at once? Suddenly, listening through T.C.'s ears, I heard wind chimes singing from a nearby residence. The last tips that flashed through my mind were the numbers forty-three and eighty-five. I felt T.C. was between these two house numbers.

I called Susie and told her what I had received from T.C. and urged her to look for him close to home immediately.

Susie and her son covered the entire area around her house, but found no T.C. They called his name, but there was no familiar response. Frantically, she began to grope through the bushes and heard something move. Susie dove in deeper, and suddenly a horribly frightened feline shot straight up into the air. He ran at top speed down the street for a couple of blocks. Susie and her son tried to keep him in sight as they began the chase.

Meanwhile, I was anxiously waiting for a call to find out what had happened. Finally, it came. "Jacquelin, this is Susie. We found T.C. He's home. I couldn't have found him without your help. Thank you so much. I'm so thankful."

Two days later, after Susie settled down, we went over all the information I had received from T.C. It hadn't registered on her at the time that her neighbors lived in a white, wooden house with a yellow awning adjacent to the door. The house number was sixty-three. T.C. had been sandwiched between the dense bushes and a cracked cement foundation. The wind chimes I had heard were at the house two doors down.

The confusing image I had received of T.C. first being close by and then being several streets away was explained by what happened when Susie finally found him after he had run from his hiding place to another yard two blocks away.

Experiences such as this one with T.C. and Susie have inspired me to help others locate their lost animal friends.

Locating an Animal

WHEN SOMEONE CALLS me to locate their missing animal, I ask them questions, such as: Have you called the animal shelters? Have you put up flyers? Where have you looked for your animal companion? Have you called the veterinarians in the area? I ask them if they have visualized their animal companion coming home. After questions are answered then I begin my process of locating their animal friend.

Before I begin to track a missing animal, I get quiet, centered, and grounded. I always tell the person that there are no guarantees and that I can only do my best. Then I set my intention to find their animal.

It takes a great deal of focus to do this work. It can be challenging, since the person and animal are usually upset. I ask the person to take a deep breath and to be as calm as they can in order to help their animal calm down, too, since they are usually traumatized. Taking time to do this allows all of our energies to be aligned, and to be clear in our intention to locate the animal. If upset continues, it can interfere with finding an animal.

Then I start tracking the animal. I communicate with the animal to see if she is in her body, astral traveling, or has crossed over into the light.

I look through an animal's eyes and tap into her memory. I communicate with the personality as well as with the soul of the animal to see what information it might give me.

I usually start tracking from the moment she left her house or premises, and get a picture of the direction she went and the route she's taking, and then pinpoint where she is in the present.

The longer an animal has been gone the more challenging it can be to locate them. This isn't always true, but it is easier to find animals who haven't been missing too long.

WHEN PEOPLE CALL ME to locate their animal companions, I will ask them what compass direction their front door faces. This way, I can tell the person what direction their animal friend has gone and is heading toward.

On paper, I sketch the person's house and label the directions, draw landmarks and streets to give me a sense of order. I always do an aerial view of the area which allows me to see landmarks.

The compass directions allow the person and me to be on the same page. For example, I might say to someone, "Your cat, Bandit, escaped out the front door heading north. I see that he's crossed six streets and then turned east. He went east for about three blocks and then turned south," and so on.

I try to be as exact as I can with directions, distances, details, and landmarks.

I LOOK FOR AS MANY DETAILS and specifics as I can find when locating a missing animal. This way, the person can keep an eye out for these objects or landmarks that

I see around the animal. For example, I might hear chimes or see the animal hanging out around a yellow house that has a blue car in the driveway. I might see a store on the corner of the street where the animal is and that there's a two-lane street in front of it.

MARGIE CALLED ME because her thirteen-year-old dog Glory had wandered away from home one evening. Glory was nearly blind so of course Margie was very concerned.

When I communicated with Glory, she showed me that she was in a kennel at a veterinarian's office.

Then, the street name flashed through my mind. I said to Margie, "Check with the veterinarian's office on South Third Avenue." She called them and sure enough, Glory was there. Someone had found Glory and taken her to this veterinarian's office, and he was trying to find out who she belonged to.

Margie told the veterinarian about the consult, and he was transformed into a believer in animal communication. He and I met for lunch a couple weeks later.

JEFF CALLED ME to help locate his lost cat Spitfire, who had been gone for over a week. As I communicated with Spitfire, she showed me the route she had been taking during the last week. I told Jeff that she had been wandering through some old rundown buildings a couple streets behind his house.

As I followed Spitfire's route, I could see that she had circled around the buildings a couple times, but was now in an old house somewhere nearby. She was frightened and in the dark. I suggested to Jeff that he check all old, abandoned houses near his residence. I felt Spitfire was close by. He checked several houses but said he didn't find her. He said there was one house that he wasn't able to get into because it was locked. A day later he called me to tell me the miracle that had just happened.

"When I was sitting at home, I realized that I used to take care of the old house that I couldn't get into for a friend of mine. It was many years ago. Anyway, I suddenly remembered I had a key to the house. I went over and got into the house and called for Spitfire. I didn't hear any response, so I was turning to leave when I heard a meow.

"I was looking everywhere for her, but couldn't find her. She meowed louder and I finally found her stuck in a dark crawl space. She couldn't get out. I couldn't believe I found her. I brought her home right away.

"What a miracle! That old key was sitting in a drawer for years. This is an absolute miracle."

Jeff and I and Spitfire rejoiced that she had been saved and was now safe. Jeff and I had prayed for divine intervention to bring his beloved Spitfire home. Divine intervention and synchronicity is exactly what happened. I always feel honored and joyful to be a part of such wondrous happenings.

MARILYN FROM NEW HAMPSHIRE called me, frantic that her lizard Jonah had gotten lost. "I had him in his backyard pen and when I went out to see how he was doing, he was gone. I'm worried because it gets cold at night and I'm afraid he might not survive."

There was an old stone wall around her yard. I gulped when I realized he had crawled inside the stone wall. I told Marilyn that he was in the west wall of her yard. She went out and looked the best she could but could not find him. Yet I knew he was there.

She told me Jonah loved bathing in the sunlight, so I suggested that she put some of his food and water in the yard so as to encourage him to come into the light.

I communicated with Jonah and asked him to come out from the stones. I showed him a picture of his food and water. He didn't come out that day, but a day later Marilyn called me. "Guess what? He just came out of the wall and into the yard where I placed his food and water. I'm so grateful, I was worried he'd die in the wall."

Prayer and Visualization

I'M A BIG BELIEVER in the power of prayer and visualization. Focusing our energies in these ways helps support an animal in whatever way they might need at the time.

Many people contact me from around the world to pray for animal companions. They ask for prayer because their dog is going in for surgery, or because their cat has crossed over, or for a behavior issue, or because their beloved friend is lost.

The following story illustrates what prayer and visualization can do to help a lost animal.

SYLVIA CALLED ME from North Carolina because her feline friend Cinnamon had run out of the house and hadn't been seen for two weeks. Cinnamon is a fourteen-year-old indoor cat.

I followed Cinnamon's steps psychically from the moment she had left to where she was presently. I gave Sylvia specifics about the area where Cinnamon was so she could go and try to find her. But I also told Sylvia she was on the move, which made this more challenging.

Sylvia drove to the area, but didn't find her beloved friend. I suggested she look in the same area for a couple days, but Cinnamon wasn't to be found. Sylvia asked me to do another consult in order to continue tracking her. When I tuned in, I could tell Cinnamon was moving in a circle, as I have found a number of cats doing when I am tracking them. She had traveled about half of a circle from Sylvia's home.

At this point, I suggested to Sylvia that she and I meditate and pray to pull Cinnamon home. She and I joined together in prayer to pull Cinnamon home. I asked Sylvia to be calm as we did this. Otherwise Cinnamon could have picked up her fear and worry, which could cause more upset.

The visual image I gave Sylvia was to imagine herself as a magnet and/or to also imagine a beam of light that extended from her heart to Cinnamon to draw her home.

I asked Sylvia to visualize Cinnamon meowing at the back door. Animals feel this energy and it helps to draw them home. I asked Sylvia to do this a few times a day. Meanwhile, I showed Cinnamon the path that would help her get home.

Sylvia called me three days later. "Oh, you won't believe it, Cinnamon showed up at my door late last night. She meowed and I ran to the door. I picked her up and held her for a long time."

We were elated that Cinnamon had completed the circle and was home in Sylvia's arms.

"MY CAT ZENA got out the door; can you help me find her?" Joanne was frantic. Her cat companion had been gone for a week.

The minute I connected with Zena, I could feel and see her wandering in a field. Zena had been having so much fun that she had lost her way. Joanne went out to look for her but could not find her. I told Joanne that I felt she would be coming home in three days when the moon was full, and to watch for her.

I asked Joanne to be like a magnet to draw her home.

Three nights later, Joanne sat in her living room meditating as she waited for Zena to arrive home. Zena sauntered up to and pawed on the screen door about 3:00 a.m.

GLORIA CALLED ME from Connecticut to see if I could locate her lost cat, Bugaboo. He had been missing for two weeks. Gloria said, "Bugaboo comes home every night so I'm not sure if he's still alive. We live beside a huge and thick wooded area."

I located Bugaboo and looked through his eyes. He was in the woods with an injured leg and couldn't get home. I told Gloria to go look for him. It was challenging to get any specific landmarks, but I tried to pinpoint the area where he was at. Gloria called me a day later to tell me that she hadn't found him.

When I checked in on Bugaboo again, he was still alive but wouldn't be for much longer.

I suggested we pray. Gloria and I joined together in prayer and asked for the miracle that Bugaboo would somehow be found or be able to come home. We prayed for divine intervention.

Gloria called me an hour later. She was so excited, she could hardly talk. "Oh, my gosh, you won't believe this. It's a miracle! I was in the kitchen and opened my refrigerator door and when I turned around, Bugaboo was standing there at the back door looking at me. I ran out and let him in the kitchen. I picked him up and hugged him. My husband was freaked by the sudden appearance of Bugaboo and ran into another room. And as I hugged Bugaboo he smelled like roses and the scent of roses filled the kitchen."

We started to laugh and agreed that this was an "honest-to-God" miracle.

When I asked Bugaboo what had happened, he communicated that Mother Mary had appeared, healed his body, and transported him home, all in a flash.

Gloria and I celebrated and thanked Mary for her divine intervention. As Gloria and I talked, we discovered that both of us had independently asked Mary to intervene. And the scent of roses is often a sign that Mary is around.

I am of no particular religious denomination, but learned many years ago that Mary watches over the animals.

Whenever I work, I always ask the angels, Mary, and other beings of light for help.

Astral Traveling

Sometimes, it's a challenge to discern if an animal has crossed over into the light or is simply astral traveling. Most of the time I can tell the difference simply due to years of experience, but no one can be a hundred percent certain. This is especially true when locating lost animals.

I learned a great deal about this when Gweyn called me from Indiana about their office cat, George. He had been living in their company's office for about a week when he simply disappeared. Everyone assumed he had scooted out the door with one of the employees. Maybe he was dead. After listening to Gweyn, I contacted George and saw him in a park, which was a couple blocks from their office building. She went and looked for him but didn't find him.

I tuned in again, and had a different experience. The image that flashed through my mind was of George being in a box somewhere in the dark. I told Gweyn I thought he was in their warehouse but was astral traveling in the park.

The next day, Gweyn called to tell me they had found George hiding in a box in the corner of the warehouse. We celebrated his being found.

Alive?

Sometimes, when people call me to find their missing animal they'll comment that they think their animal is dead. I have worked with numerous people to validate, unfortunately, that I felt their intuition was correct. But sometimes if an animal is astral traveling, it may seem like they're dead. They're traveling to a place that may be more pleasant than where their body is currently. If an animal is very scared, they can dissociate just like a person. They're floating around their body, rather than being fully present in their body.

I will ask the animals if they're occupying their bodies. Some say yes, some say no, while others are confused and say they don't know. I ask the Spirit for clarification.

Also, I look around to see where the animal is because that might give me a clue.

It's not unusual for an animal who dies suddenly to fail to realize that they're dead.

It can be challenging to sort this out, and all any animal communicator can do is his or her best.

JANE CALLED ME because her dog Pete had been missing for four days, which was unusual. Jane had attended my workshops and was trying to communicate with Pete, but could not get a connection.

When I asked Pete to show me where he was, his spirit appeared and told me that he had gotten killed by a coyote.

Jane said she felt he had been killed but didn't want to accept it. She searched for his body but never found it. And Pete never returned home. Jane and I blessed and released his spirit into the hands of God.

Finding a Frightened/Shy Animal

IT IS ALWAYS MORE CHALLENGING to recover a shy or frightened animal than one who is friendly and outgoing. I've located many frightened, shy animals who could not respond to their name being called by their person or to food being put down for them.

I do not give up on the shy animals; it simply takes more patience and communicating with the animal to help.

When I communicate with a lost animal, I always ask him to come out of hiding and show his body to his person or to a friendly human who might be able to help them find their way home. I have found this request to help animals be recovered.

Stay Where You Are/Show Your Body

WHEN I DO A CONSULT with someone to locate their lost animal companion, I ask the animal to remain where he is and tell him that his person is coming to look for him. When I do this, I tell the person not to try and draw their animal home at the same time, because the animal starts moving in response to the person's energy. I ask the person to look for their animal for a couple of days before trying to draw the animal home through visualization.

PAULA CALLED ME about her dog Stan. She had let him out of the car to run in a field that was surrounded by woods. Paula had brought Stan to this field many times, but this time he had taken off and she couldn't find him.

"I'm frantic. I went into the woods and looked all over and couldn't find him. I think he's dead or someone stole him. Please help."

When I communicated with Stan, he was in his body and showed me that he was running around in the woods. I did an overview of the area psychically to see what specific landmarks I could give her. I told her I saw two streets that ran along the wooded area. I told her I felt Stan would come out on one of those two streets.

I asked Stan to return to the field and communicated to him that Paula would be coming to look for him. I asked him to stay put, but to show his body to Paula so she could see him.

The next day Paula drove to one of the streets and looked for him. But no Stan. Then she drove to the other street. Within two minutes of her driving by the field, Stan popped out of the woods. She called to him, and he ran into her arms. They were elated to see each other.

On the Move

IT CAN BE CHALLENGING to recover an animal who's on the move. I may locate where an animal is at a given moment, but by the time the person gets there the animal has vanished.

Sometimes I will try and move ahead in time to see if I can intuit where the animal may be heading. Sometimes this works and other times it doesn't.

Let Go

WHEN A PERSON'S beloved animal companion is missing, it can be difficult for them to "loosen" their grasp on the animal.

I usually will say to the person I'm working with, "As hard as it is, let go and trust that God or the Universe is in control. Let's ask God to reunite you two. Let's ask for divine intervention." This frees up the energies of the person and animal so the Universe can work it out.

In the end, there is a bigger picture going on with the person and their animal friend that they can't see and might not ever see or understand as to why their animal is found or not.

JUDY CALLED from Florida to see if I could track her beloved Rottweiler, Mac. She had put flyers out all over town. Three people had seen him, but he was constantly on the run, which made it challenging to recover him.

Judy had a number of people out looking for him. She even had an ad on television, showing Mac and offering a reward to give the community incentive to find her friend.

I located him more than once. I'd give the location to Judy, and someone would spot him in the area I had mentioned, but by the time she or someone else she knew got there, he had disappeared.

He communicated to me that he had gotten lost and wanted to come home, but couldn't stop moving. Finally, Judy caught up with Mac a week later. This had a happy ending.

Do All Animals Want to Be Found?

WHEN PEOPLE CALL me to locate a lost, beloved animal companion, I do my best to locate them and to help the person recover them.

Most of the animals I communicate with desire to be found. Some animals slip out the door, wander around, and end up getting lost. Others may jump a backyard fence, run off to have an adventure, and not be able to find their way home. I receive many calls from people who have recently moved to a new house whose animals go outside and can't find their way home. And then there are animals who run away from home and do not want to be found.

ANIMALS I'VE COMMUNICATED WITH have given me some of the following reasons for leaving home.

- The animal's running away because their person isn't giving them enough attention.
- There's a new animal in the house that they don't get along with and/or feel they're displaced or replaced.
- When a new animal is brought into a household, many animals have communicated the following question to me: "Who asked me if I wanted another animal here?"
- They can't tolerate the energy of people arguing in a household, or some other circumstance in the home.
- Some move on because their mission where they were has been completed, and they're moving on to a new mission with someone else.
- Animals may leave when a divorce or death occurs, depending on the circumstances and people's energies.

• Animals may take themselves out of their body, for example getting hit by a car. This is because they have completed their mission on Earth and it's time to return to spirit form.

PAM CALLED ME because her cat, Sienna, had disappeared from her household. Sienna was an indoor/outdoor cat who usually came home promptly at dinner time. But he had not shown up for days.

When I communicated with Sienna, he said,"I'm not coming back home. Three other cats in the household was already overwhelming for me. And now there are four. No one asked me about this. There's not enough space for all of us."

I shared this with Pam and she asked me to ask Sienna if he would come back if she found the new kitty another home. Sienna and I conversed awhile. I asked him if he would be willing to at least try to adjust to the new cat, with another option being that Pam would find him another home. He said he had just had it and was moving on to find himself a home with fewer cats. There was nothing I could say to change his mind, and it didn't feel right to try further. So Pam blessed and released him.

IT'S IMPORTANT TO REMEMBER that animals make their own choices from both the personality and soul level. It's not always about what we want or what we think is best for them.

If an animal decides they are ready to leave their home with us, then we must respect that choice and release them. And if the soul has decided to pull its spirit out of the body because it is ready to do so, the animal will find a way to be released from her body.

ANNA CALLED ME from Oregon about her cat Herman, who had been missing for a week. I located him a few miles away from her house and asked him to stay where he was so Anna could come and find him. He responded with, "No, tell her to not bother looking for me. I will hide."

I was puzzled by this response and asked Anna about what was going on in her household. She told me that she had been keeping Herman in a cage for many months, because she was afraid her beagle Tommy might bite or kill him.

Herman had been very unhappy being caged up every day when Anna was at work and Tommy had the run of the house.

I suggested to Anna that if she recovered Herman, to possibly kennel Tommy rather than Anna, since cats do not like to be caged. Herman communicated that he hated it. She said she would be willing to try this. I communicated her message to Herman, but he said he didn't want to live in her household any longer.

It is difficult to share this kind of message with people, but again, animals have the right to make their own choices.

Lessons

WHETHER I FIND a person's animal companion or not, I like to ask the question, "Is there some kind of lesson here?" The person will think about this and then we discuss their feelings and insights. This seems to give meaning to what has happened, and from this emerges growth for the person and animal.

I ALWAYS FEEL HONORED and joyful when the divine uses me as a conduit to be a part of helping someone find their animal companion. It's amazing how the Universe orchestrates and synchronizes everything in order for animals to be reunited with their people. There truly is a divine order, not only in locating lost animals, but with all that is within the Universe and beyond.

What You Can Do

HERE ARE GUIDELINES that will help you locate and/or attract your animal companion home.

Most people go out and search for their animal companions when they turn up missing. They'll put up flyers and look in places where they think their animal might have run off to.

Before You Go Look For Your Animal Companion

Heart Connection

Step 1. Sit in a quiet place.

Step 2. Center and breathe, being present in mind and body. Set your intention to connect with your animal friend.

Step 3. Radiate light from your heart to the animal's heart creating a heart-to-heart connection. Send calming energy to your animal friend to help her quiet down.

Step 4. Ask your animal friend if she's lost or has run away from home. If she's run away ask her why. If she's not happy for some reason, try and work this out with her.

Step 5. Ask your animal to show you which way she went. Did she run out the front or back door? Did she turn right or left? How far away is she? Ask her about what kind of objects she sees. For example, if she's by a house, ask her what color the house is. Ask if there's a car in the driveway and what color. Ask her what sounds she's hearing. Are there people around and has anyone been feeding her? If so, what does the person look like? Ask her if she's trapped somewhere and if so, ask her what she senses or remembers is around her. Is she injured? Can she travel?

Step 6. Tell your animal to stay put and to show her body when she hears, sees, or senses you.

Step 7. Ask for divine intervention. Ask your angels and her angels to guide and reunite you.

Step 8. Go look for your animal. Early morning can be a good time to look for animals because there are fewer people out and about. Twilight can also be a good time to look as the day quiets down. As you look, continue to connect with her off and on so you can get a sense of where she is.

Step 9. Continue to look for your animal friend. Thank God and the Universe for answering your prayers.

Step 10. Visualize both of you being reunited. Then release your prayers to the Universe so they can flow with your intention.

After you have looked for your animal companion for a few days, I recommend doing the Magnetic Heart of Love Technique. In most instances, I do not recommend doing this technique after initially communicating and getting a sense of where your animal is because animals usually start moving again. The Magnetic Heart of Love Technique draws them home.

If an animal is very close to home, I will sometimes recommend to someone that they do the Heart Connection Technique and go look for their animal during the day and early evening and then do the Magnetic Heart of Love Technique during the evening.

Magnetic Heart of Love Technique

Follow the first three steps in the Heart Connection, then:

Step 4. Imagine that the light of love within your heart is a magnet that will draw your animal friend home. Do this two or three times daily for five to ten minutes. You don't want to do this with a "grasping" energy, but with an openness that allows the Universe's energies to flow with your intention.

Step 5. Visualize your animal friend sitting at the door or window she usually uses when she goes outside. Hear her meowing or barking, clawing at the door, and so on. If your animal isn't an outdoor animal, visualize her at the door she might lie behind.

Step 6. Ask for divine intervention. Ask your angels and your animal's guardian angels to reunite you. And then affirm, "I release this into the hands of God and the Universe."

Step 7. Thank God and the Universe for answering your prayers and then release the prayers so the universal energy can flow to do its work.

Release

IT CAN BE CHALLENGING for us to connect with our animal companion because we are so emotionally close to them. Yet everyone has the intuitive ability to communicate with animals and can help draw their beloved animal home if they have gotten lost.

When your animal friend returns home, there's great joy for all concerned. But if she doesn't return home, then there are reasons why. Perhaps her mission with you is done or she is ready to leave this plane.

It's challenging to try and understand all the "whys," and I don't think we ever can.We can only do our best and then release our animal friend and the circumstance into God's hands.

Chapter Twelve

Soul Recovery for Animals

THE POWERFUL WORK of SR involves gathering the pieces of an animal's soul and/or pieces of their energy bodies that have fragmented due to emotional and/or physical trauma and integrating them back into their proper place so that the animal's mind, body, emotions, and soul are once again intact and aligned. The animal experiences "wholeness" once again. Each fragment carries a part of the animal's life force. So when all parts come "home" (I'm borrowing Ingerman's term "home" in referring to the body), the animal can fulfill their potential and live a happier, healthier life.

Some animals fragment early in life while others fragment later on due to trauma. SR work can be compared to putting the pieces of a jigsaw puzzle together.

After doing SR with animals for a short time, I was stunned by the immediate results people saw in their animal companions. I knew this work was important.

It isn't any surprise that animals need SR. Animals are subjected to our stress, violence, and fast-paced lives. They fracture more often than we might want to admit.

I BECAME INTERESTED in Soul Recovery around 1991. I first began guiding humans with SR and decided to try this work with animals. Before '91, I had experienced Michael Harner's techniques of shamanic journey and journeyed on a regular basis into various dimensions (or worlds) for my own healing. Someone would rattle while I journeyed or I'd put on an audio tape of rattling. Then I read Sandra Ingerman's book *Soul Retrieval*, which made perfect sense and opened doors into the work I was doing with people and animals.

I've experienced SR work personally. Several practitioners helped me to retrieve lost parts of myself that had flown off during several traumatic events. I was also involved in a group for a few years, led by anthropologist Felicitas Goodman, Ph.D., who discovered that various body postures, used by shamans worldwide, could carry one into a trance state to experience a shamanic journey. For example, one posture would be used for healing, another for insight, and so on. She'd rattle while the group journeyed.

Through the years, the angels have taught and guided me to do this work in ways that work well. Most of my work is done over the telephone, so I no longer listen to an audio tape of a rattle while doing SR. After praying and setting an intention for the work, I find myself instantly present in other dimensions, seeing where I need to begin. But there are occasions when the animal is physically present with me at my office during SR.

This chapter is *not* intended to teach anyone how to do SR, so please don't try SR on your own. Anyone who desires to do this work should receive appropriate training from an experienced SR practitioner. Here, I want to share the almost miraculous results I've seen happen from doing this work.

When Fragmentation Occurs

ANIMALS CAN BECOME fragmented in many ways, such as: birth trauma, physical abuse (being kicked or hit), emotional abuse (being screamed at), abandoned, hit by a car, getting lost, near-death experience, surgery, illness, pain, and fearful and/or stressful experiences, abuse that takes place while being trained or tamed. (Many horses are shadows of who they truly are.)

An Italian greyhound pup Sasha, born with neurological challenges, fragmented because she was frightened her first day at clicker training. She showed me ten big dogs in class, especially one who scared her. Sasha was the smallest dog there. It was her first time socializing with more than one dog at a time. Her person said, "Sasha shook like the Earth was going to end." And that's exactly how she felt. Sasha's person was surprised to hear she had fragmented from a clicker training class, but seeing the class through Sasha's eyes, I could understand why.

A young woman called me to work with her cat Sally, who had been kicked in the head by an angry man. He had caused so much damage that Sally had to have surgery and she almost died. When I checked in with her, I saw a number of pieces that had been literally "kicked" out of her bodies. After doing SR work, the woman said Sally acted more present and seemed to be in less pain. Sally used to hiss at one particular cat in the household, but after the SR work she stopped hissing and had begun to actually warm up to him.

Symptoms

AN ANIMAL IN NEED of SR work will often seem scattered and as if "they're not all there." That's because they're not. And they will usually exhibit a variety of problems and/or misbehaviors. They may be ungrounded, trip over objects, appear dreamy, seem distracted, act imbalanced, or experience illnesses. They may suffer from separation anxiety, depression, aggression, phobias, and other symptoms.

Getting to the Root

MOST PHYSICAL AND BEHAVIORAL problems begin in the spirit, which directly affects the energy bodies and in turn manifests in the physical body. So why not go to the root of the problem?

In doing this work, I find that fragments need to be integrated into the etheric bodies (emotional, mental, and spirit bodies) as well as the physical body and soul.

As I do this work, I look at an animal's basic energetic blueprint clairvoyantly in order to integrate fragments into their proper place. All the bodies and soul are a complex network of energies. When a fragment comes home, it has wonderful benefits for the whole animal.

This healing work creates positive change that occurs in the physical body, energy bodies, mind, emotions, and spirit. I find this is so no matter what the reason for fragmentation. For instance, I've worked with animals who were nearly knocked out of their bodies and fragmented when kicked hard or hit by a car; others were screamed at or abandoned. SR helped all of them. It improves an animal's overall well-being and behavior.

Angels

IN ALL THE WORK I do with animals, I always ask the animal's guardian angels, other angels, and light beings to direct and guide me as well as my intuitive self. I'm an instrument they work through, and I guess you could say it's a team effort.

The angels clear the fragments and help heal them as they integrate each one into its proper place. I listen closely as they direct me in this work. Also, I listen to the animal's soul, which communicates what needs to be done in order for healing to take place.

As the angels work, I hear heavenly music and watch flashing neon rainbows heal the animals. There's celebration in the heavens and within the heart and soul of the animal and me when she is restored to wholeness.

Some animals are more fragmented than others. I'm careful and do SR step by step. I've discovered that there's an order that is beneficial and sometimes necessary in order for all parts to return and integrate properly. I feel this order intuitively, and listen to the angels so that all parts integrate back into place. I watch, clairvoyantly, each part integrate. If a part doesn't want to integrate for some reason, then I spend time talking with that part to help it see that there's a better place for it to be. I'll show it where home is, within the animal's energy bodies.

Beginning SR

I MEDITATE and have certain rituals I like to do before beginning an SR. I say prayers and this sets the intention for healing and wholeness to be restored for the animal. Then my vision (or part of my awareness) travels to other dimensions where the angels and I meet. Here I am shown what I need to see and know. There's no time or space in other dimensions, so I am able to do what I need to do in order to assist the animal.

Sometimes, I'm shown issues that need to be addressed before or during SR.

For example, there might be something or someone who's trying to block this process, or effects from past lives that need to be dealt with, or fears that need to be understood and released.

It may take more than one session, and often does when deep fragmentation has occurred. The following encounters will give you a feel for the healing power of SR work.

Java

JAVA'S PERSON CAROL called me in regard to separation anxiety and several other problems, including that one of his eyes was crossed. Java had been rescued from a man who had been beating him and was going to shoot him. This man had shot and killed Java's brother in front of him.

Because of the severe abuse, Java was fragmented. Parts of his energy bodies had departed during the abuse in order to survive and stay sane. (People often do the same thing during severe abuse.) With gentleness, guidance, and help from Java's guardian angels, Java showed me all the trauma, which could then be released from his mind and spirit, losing power over him.

I did three sessions with Java. The angels and I retrieved and integrated the pieces of his energy bodies into place. There were parts of his mind, third eye, heart, legs, and spirit that had fragmented and scattered in various other dimensions.

I explained to every part of Java telepathically that the past was over and wouldn't be repeated. By my stating this, his fragments softened, and the angels soothed them, which allowed integration to then go smoothly.

A minute or so after the first session, after a few of the pieces of Java were back in place, I told Carol that his eyes changed and should look clear. She squealed, "I was just going to tell you that his eyes are now normal—the one that was crossed is now normal. His eyes are bright." I asked her to put her hand gently over his third eye and say, "Welcome home; we all need clear sight."

Because most consults are by phone, I ask the animal's person to place their hand over the particular area where the fragment has integrated and to say "welcome home," and to repeat a phrase that I receive intuitively to strengthen, comfort, or reassure parts in the following weeks. This helps the pieces or energies to remain integrated and heal. Most people love being involved in their animal's recovery in this way.

In the weeks that followed the third session, Carol told me Java was a different dog. He was friendlier, more confident, and happy. She said he walked with a bounce and had a deeper, fuller bark. A number of Carol's friends noticed the changes, and she had not mentioned the work that had been done. It was inspiring to see him whole and enjoying life. Integration happens over a period of time, but I often see immediate results like Java's.

After a Session

RIGHT AFTER DOING an SR session, some animals will sleep, others will have loads of energy. Every animal is different. A friend of mine asked me to do SR for a dog she had found wandering in the street. He was in bad shape, but was improving little by little. There were six parts of Sam that had taken off in order for him to survive. Before the SR, my friend said he wouldn't play with any toys. She called me the day after the session to say he had started to play with his toys. He looked happier and seemed to be at peace.

Joey

MY EXPERIENCE WITH JOEY shows how parts of the self can be resistant, even when the soul and personality is crying out for wholeness.

Joey, a sixty-pound shepherd mix, came to me broken-hearted. His person Jill loved him deeply and felt I could help him. When he was nine months old she rescued him from the hands of an abuser. Joey had been severely abused—his left front leg had been broken and never cared for, so it healed in a way he could no longer bend his elbow or paw. He had been burned with cigarettes. It was one of the worst cases I've ever seen. Joey communicated how sad and depressed he was and how hard it was for him to walk some days. I picked up that he was suffering from post-traumatic stress disorder. I asked Jill if he startled easily and she said, "Yes." Also, I mentioned that Joey told me he had nightmares. Jill said that confirmed her hunch, since his sleep seemed so restless.

I told her the abuser's actions had been unpredictable, so that even today any sudden movements could trigger off Joey's memories and fears. Jill confirmed this.

I asked Joey telepathically if he wanted to be whole again. He shouted, "Yes!" This makes the work much easier. So, I asked him to dump out and let go of the painful memories. I viewed his memories, like a movie, in order to pick up key emotions that might need to be worked with later on.

Joey was only alive because he had left his body, he had a strong will, and because Jill rescued him. In watching his memories, I could also tell Jill what triggered him emotionally and how to deal with it. I often recommend a number of Bach Flower Remedies to help support the SR work and to handle any emotional residue from the session.

So, I began the SR with asking the angels, Joey's soul, and his guardian angels to guide this work. I could see right away that Joey had a number of parts that had left in order for him to survive mentally and physically.

Joey wanted the fragments to come home, but his fragments weren't sure they wanted to return to his body. I spent time explaining to the fragments that they were a part of Joey's bodies. Healing and happiness couldn't happen without their cooperation. I explained to them that they held feelings and memories, but that they'd be safe now. The abuse was over. The abuser was gone.

We started with the third eye. When this fragment returns in any animal, the eyes are suddenly clear and sparkle. They may even change color. It's as if a veil has been lifted from their eyes and they literally see things more clearly. They adjust to their new sight quickly. His third eye came back rather easily after cleansing it with light.

Then we went on to Joey's head. Trauma was still attached to this part, so I asked the angels to clear and cleanse it away as I watched more traumatic memories pass before my eyes. As the head fragment started to integrate, it pulled away. When this happens, I stop and find out what's going on. I asked for insight. Joey's terror and anger was keeping this part bound to the abuser. I told Joey and his head piece that if he wanted to be free and whole, he'd have to let go and forgive. The man was gone and wouldn't ever hurt him again. Joey was able to forgive and release the abuser. Then this part integrated smoothly into the mental body.

Then we moved to the heart fragment. This part practically flew back into Joey's emotional and physical bodies and blossomed like a flower. I said to Joey, "We all need heart, don't we?" He agreed with a resounding "yes," and beamed with a heavenly light he hadn't known since shortly after birth. He's now twelve years old. I always feel a deep joy beyond words when the fragments come home and the animal remembers who he or she really is.

Next, a piece of his spirit that had bolted far away into the stars was a bit more willing to come back after watching these other parts journey home. At this point I said to Joey, "Look at what a bright, beautiful soul you are."

"Is that me?" he asked.

"Yes," I communicated. He was delighted to know that this light was truly him. The angels and I reminded him of the truth, which was that his essence is love.

He had forgotten who he was because of the severe abuse and fragmenting, but now he could see his own beauty. Then his glowing spirit settled in gently with his other bodies.

I then checked in with his legs. When his leg had been broken, both front legs split off and flew far away into the Milky Way, and they were still hiding. The angels and I talked with them and they refused to come home. So we all spent time conveying to the legs that the abuse was over and that the safest and happiest place for them to be was in Joey's body, where they had originated. This was the perfect place for them to be if they wanted safety and peace. They said they'd think about it. Several weeks later, the legs said that they'd give it a try. Joey was sitting across the room with Jill when the legs integrated. The second they integrated, he walked over to me, turned, and stood with his back against my legs. I placed my hands over his legs and whispered, "Welcome home, what strong legs you have." He was delighted all fragments were home.

I asked the angels to seal this work with love and light, which I always do after completing SR work.

Joey is clearly a "new" dog. I continue to do healing work on his spinal column and legs. His back is more aligned and he's walking in a balanced way that is also new and wonderful.

Jill tells me Joey is much happier, has more energy, is healthier, is using his legs more and able to walk further. He's even starting to use the front leg that had been broken. She said he jumped up on the couch and lay on his back, which she hadn't seen him do in many years. Sometimes Jill has to hold him back, because he feels so good and tends to overdo things. He's out of pain now and you can see light dancing in his eyes.

Past Life Influences

I'VE BEEN WORKING with a pup (Italian greyhound) with neurological problems, whom I mentioned earlier. When she first came to me she had trouble walking and her paws would knuckle under. She had a difficult time playing. At times, her body shook as if covered in snow. She had fragmented during a hard birth and had carried in quite a bit of fracturing in from past lives, especially in regard to her skull.

After doing SR, including integrating past life pieces into her past life etheric bodies, we saw marked improvement. I worked with her soul on healing past life issues that were still influencing her energetic bodies.

I continue to work on balancing her bodies, chakras, and brain rhythms with positive results. She moves better overall and now acts like a normal puppy.

Today she bounds around my office and teases me with her elephant toy. She has a great deal more energy, and she's present in every way. Her eyes shine and she's enjoying life.

Lost Souls

JOERDIE HAD TAKEN her dog companion Helios to get his teeth cleaned at the veterinarian's. When she walked him into the hospital, she heard him communicate telepathically with a little gray dog name Kara, who was going to be put to sleep shortly. He told her that he would help her cross over into the light. (I had done

Jacquelin doing SR work with Sasha.

work with Helios in the past and know him to be a highly evolved soul who helps many on this Earth plane and beyond.)

Joerdie called me because three days after having his teeth cleaned he was not acting normally. Helios was disoriented and had trouble walking. Joerdie knew he had helped Kara cross over and now he wasn't fully present. He was seeking light and stumbling around as if he were blind at times. She called the veterinarian and he said Helios was fine physically, so Joerdie was clear that something else was going on.

We both knew he was mostly out of his body. He had helped Kara cross over, but her spirit had clung to him when he tried to get back into his body. Kara wanted to stay attached to his body.

I looked at Helios clairvoyantly and saw hundreds of spirits in and around his body. What had happened was that when Helios was under anesthetic, hundreds of lost souls who were in and around the animal hospital had grabbed onto his "shirt tails" as he was helping Kara go into the light. Some of them remained in the light, but hundreds of them were still in and around Helios's bodies.

The angels and I helped the lost souls move into the light. We finally convinced Kara to go into the light after helping her resolve feelings about her person who had dropped her off at the veterinarian's to be euthanized.

I saw all kinds of animal spirits. There were cats, dogs, rabbits, a groundhog, and many others. Joerdie mentioned she had seen a groundhog lying in the street as she was driving Helios home from the veterinarian's. The groundhog had hitched a ride. After I mentioned the spirits, she said that Helios had been acting cat-like the night before.

No wonder Helios couldn't get fully back into his body. These spirits were trying to take up residence. Please understand these were not bad spirits, but simply lost souls trying to find their way home to the light.

After all the beings were ushered into the light, the angels and I brought back Helios's fragments and integrated them into place. I aligned his chakras with his high self, soul, and Creator. As this was going on, Joerdie said Helios let out a big sigh and stretched his body with relief.

I suggested that Helios drink more water to cleanse his system. She laughed. Helios had stood up and walked over to his water dish and started drinking.

This is a dramatic case showing what a big difference SR can make in an animal's life.

LINDA CALLED ME to communicate with her thoroughbred, Susie. Linda said Susie had been a race horse before coming to her. Now, she went on trail rides with Susie, but was concerned because Susie was stumbling and did not seem to be fully there. Linda also told me that Susie had a difficult time riding in a trailer. She would kick the back door of the trailer and had once hurt herself. Linda felt she needed a SR.

When I communicated with Susie, she shared with me how horrible it had been being a race horse. She said she had never wanted to race but was forced to until the trainer finally gave up on her. Susie was glad to be out of training and off the track.

From this communication I could see that she had been abused and was fragmented. I did a SR, cleared away the trauma, and brought back a number of fragments that had jetted into other realms in order to survive. Susie was willing to forgive the person who had whipped her. She welcomed the SR and was thrilled when all her fragments had been integrated. She welcomed them home. Susie beamed with joy as so many of the animals do as they regain their wholeness. Because of the trauma, she had not been able to express the essence of who she was for a very long time.

Linda called me several weeks after the SR. She said that she was able to get Susie into the trailer without any incident. Also, she said that Susie did not kick once during a two-hour trip. She also reported that Susie was no longer stumbling and was acting very present, bright eyed and confident.

What a gift for us all. I could hear the angels singing. We all celebrated Susie's healing.

JANET CALLED ME about her dog, Kiko, who had not been acting like himself since two dogs had attacked him in their backyard. Janet cried,"I dived into the middle of the dogs to protect Kiko, who's smaller than the other dogs. One of the dogs had gotten his teeth stuck in Kiko's collar and panicked. She was trying to pull away and it was choking Kiko. Kiko was going limp. I flung my body over Kiko's, and was able to get the dog's teeth released from Kiko's collar."

Fortunately, Janet came out with only a few scratches. She said that it took a few minutes for Kiko to start breathing normally again. And now he was acting spacey and depressed.

I checked him over, and he had fractured during this traumatic event. In fact, Kiko had gone through a near death experience. Also, various parts of him had scattered into other realms in order to cope during the attack.

The angels and I gathered his fragments and placed them into their appropriate places within Kiko's bodies. I did further work balancing out Kiko's chakras and reconnecting energy circuits in his brain that had gotten disconnected during the attack.

Janet contacted me a week later to let me know that Kiko was now acting present and happy. She said his eyes were bright and that he was actually acting more present and happier than before the attack.

Angus

I WAS IN A BARN presenting a workshop on telepathic communication with animals. Mary and Mary had brought their dog Angus along so I could do a private consult with him following the workshop. Angus was having trouble walking along with some other physical issues.

Angus was sitting by Mary and Mary during the workshop. At one point, I said, "So whose horse would like to volunteer to teach us communication?" In that moment, Angus stood up, walked over to me very slowly, and sat directly in front of me. He gazed into my eyes, and communicated, "I want to volunteer to help teach these people learn how to communicate with animals." We all burst out laughing because no one could believe the synchronistic timing of his actions with my question. Everyone agreed that Angus would be great to have as a teacher.

After the workshop, I did some energy adjustments and SR with Angus. Mary and Mary and others watched as his eyes actually brightened while I worked with him.

When I was done, I asked Mary to put him down on the ground. The second he was on the ground he literally ran around inside the barn. Mary and Mary could not believe that this was happening because he had been having a hard time walking very far without wobbling and had to sit down to rest from the pain. In the upcoming months Angus continued to improve.

Mary and Mary requested further SR work so I went on working with him, bringing back fractured pieces along with doing long-distance healing.

Months later, Mary and Mary called to tell me that their veterinarian had found a tumor on one of his lungs. They said his breathing was labored and that he wasn't eating much. They asked me to do whatever needed to be done to help him. I went into meditation and could see the tumor. So the angels and I cleared away the energy of the tumor and I brought back several fragments and integrated them into place. I didn't know what to expect.

Mary and Mary called me a couple days later very excited. They said that after I had worked with him he immediately took a big turn for the better. He was breathing normally again and eating well. They took him back to the veterinarian a week later to be checked over and were told that the tumor was gone! The veterinarian wanted to know what had happened and Mary and Mary told her that I had done a healing session with Angus. The veterinarian and I met two weeks later at a veterinary conference where I was speaking on nonverbal communication with animals.

Angus recently passed away due to old age. I felt honored to work with him over a period of a few years. He is a bright, amazing soul who comes to visit me now and then. It's always a pleasure to visit with him.

Results

SOUL RECOVERY WORK makes a huge difference in an animal's life. They're more present and become who they truly are, which shifts them into more normal and balanced behaviors. They feel better and are aligned with their soul.

An animal who's had SR work is more energetic, happy, healthy, and strong, and their eyes sparkle with light. Right after SR work, the first thing I check out is the eyes. They truly are the windows of the soul. Some animals' sense of smell is better; some hear more clearly. Healing takes place on many levels with this work. There's an inner harmony that wasn't present before. Some animals begin to have feeling in parts of their body that used to be numb. I had done SR on a horse named Blaze. Many pieces had left due to abuse. A few days after the SR work, his person told me that while he was being shoed, he flinched, which he had never done before. I told her that Blaze now had feeling in his back legs that once were numb. Healing happens in many ways as deeper integration takes place over weeks and months.

Animals accept SR work well and with gratitude. I don't see any major upheavals of anger, depression, or distress after doing this work as sometimes happens with humans. They process SR in a different way. Their souls and guardian angels guide the integration and healing process. I have found that modalities such as TTouch, Bach Flower Remedies, chakra balancing, and good nutrition help support the SR work.

SR work is not a replacement for medical treatment, but it adds a dimension of healing, working from the spiritual level, that is not often considered. Every animal deserves to be whole. When animals are restored to wholeness, they live up to their potential and lead happy, fulfilling lives.

I am honored to be an instrument and feel great joy in being a part of doing this wonderful work with animals.

Chapter Thirteen

Death

THIS CHAPTER MAY CHALLENGE your existing ideas about death: for instance, the idea that death is final, or that the human animal is the only animal privileged to experience eternal life. It is illogical to think that the Creator would bless only humans with souls.

If we expand our minds and hearts, we'll realize that all forms of life are the Creator's children. The Creator cares for all life forms, not just humans. All of the Universe's children, the four-leggeds, wingeds, two-leggeds, and no-legged beings, have souls.

THE PHONE RANG and when I picked it up I heard a woman sobbing "My sixteen-year-old cat Robert is ill. He's been on baby food for months because he vomits if he eats regular food. Now the baby food doesn't help and he has diarrhea."

Robert had been seen by a veterinarian various times, but Marilyn wanted to know what he was thinking and feeling.

As I communicated with Robert, I could sense his dizziness. He was staggering rather than walking. When I asked Marilyn if she was seeing this she said, "Yes, he's staggering like he's dizzy." Robert went on with, "I'm old, tired, and in pain. I've had a good life and it's time for me to go. Let me go in dignity."

As I heard his silent message, I asked if there was anything we could do for him. His response was, "No, just let me go."

The next day Marilyn took Robert to the veterinarian to find out his present physical state. The veterinarian strongly recommended Robert be euthanized because he wouldn't be able to recover from his deteriorating condition. As Marilyn told me about the visit she kept saying, "But I can't put him to sleep; he's my whole life."

I told her I understood how she felt but that she needed to consider Robert's wishes. She said, "I need tonight to think about it." The next day she had Robert put to sleep. We talked about him and all the emotions she was experiencing. Several days later Marilyn asked me if animals had souls, and if I could contact Robert.

As we talked I contacted Robert's presence and knew he was feeling relief and peace. He was happy to be released from the continual pain. I could feel a warm, quiet smile from the depth of his being. I shared Robert's feelings with Marilyn and she said, "I feel he's happy and finally at peace."

We talked a number of times during the next few weeks. At times she expressed guilt and anger, other times fear and grief. Marilyn was slowly accepting and adjusting to the tremendous loss of Robert.

EMOTIONS CAN BE COMPLEX when processing death. I assist many people with the grief process. I've been through it myself a number of times and know how challenging it can be.

A variety of emotions emerge when animal friends die: everything from denial, anger, and guilt to depression, sorrow, and fear. Here are a few reasons why: Denial and anger over an animal's death because the animal is gone and the person wasn't able to prevent the death. Guilt over euthanasia or circumstances of death, "If I had been watching him, he wouldn't have run into the street and been killed by a car." There can be depression from the loss, the changes, emptiness, and unexpressed feelings. Sorrow over the loss and for the self. There can be a fear of being without the animal who filled many needs and who so freely gave comfort and a sense of security, love, and affection.

It's important to feel, express, and understand these emotions before we truly can let them go. This takes time and talking to someone who is caring and supportive.

The deeper feelings underlying loss can sometimes stem from fear and anger at not being able to control unpredictable death that sooner or later embraces every living thing. Some fear death is final, yet wonder if there are souls that do survive physical death. Does life go on after the body dies, even though most people don't sense this dimension?

Animal friends fill our lives with great riches. They offer genuine love, joy, spontaneity, affection, and companionship. So why do we wonder if it's normal to feel devastated when they are gone from our lives? Some people call me and say,

"I'm embarrassed because I'm shattered over an animal," or "People will think I'm crazy if they know how upset I am." Unfortunately, our society doesn't consider grieving over an animal acceptable. Those who have never had a close relationship with an animal may have a hard time understanding all this.

IT'S DIFFICULT TO DEAL with the reactions of people after you lose a family member who happens to be a dog, cat, horse, rabbit, bird, or guinea pig. They aren't just pets but treasured brothers, sisters, and friends.

One friend of mine looked at me in amazement when I cried and talked about missing my cat companion Bella, who had to be euthanized. "It was just a pet. Go get another one. Besides, you have another cat at home." Her response shocked me.

People who have never been in a close relationship with an animal may make comments like my friend's. The best way to deal with the situation during this painful time is to seek out people who love and live with animals for support during and, if possible, to be with those who truly empathize because they have experienced the loss of a beloved animal friend

Through the years, I have communicated with many dying animals. I've learned a great deal about dying, death, and grief from animals as well as their people. It is very important for people to accept, express, and understand their grief.

The loss of an animal companion can feel more devastating and intense when the animal friend was a person's most significant relationship, which was the case with Marilyn. Robert was the center of her life. It's easy to become dependent on an animal for fulfilling numerous needs. Animals greet us joyfully at the door when we come home, listen to our woes, love us no matter what we say or do, and are loyal, constant companions.

What Does Your Animal Companion Want?

BECAUSE WE CAN TELEPATHICALLY communicate with animals, it's of the utmost importance to listen to what an animal wants concerning life and death decisions. Let us not base decisions on what is easiest for us or what lessens our pain. If an animal has an incurable disease or an ongoing, serious condition, we must give them the right to decide how far we are to go in saving them, how long they want to live, and how and when they choose to end their life on Earth.

Every animal I've communicated with has unique feelings, wishes, and questions about their particular situation. Animals think about how and when to leave their physical bodies, and desire to be given a choice.

Requests I hear from animals, again and again, who are getting ready to leave the body are: "If the pain gets any worse I do not wish to go on."

"If I can't get better I don't want to live."

"I wish to die naturally, but if the pain becomes unbearable I want to be put to sleep."

"I am ready to go."

"I want to die at home with my person embracing me."

BETTY TALKED TO ME about her cat Harry, who was fourteen years old and living with her former husband in their old house. He wasn't eating well and was moving toward kidney failure. He had recently been through the stress of his peoples' divorce.

Harry was absorbing Richard's emotional pain, anger, and confusion over a divorce he didn't want. Betty and I discussed Harry moving in to her apartment, but Harry felt it best to stay where he was since he was getting ready to die. He said he had begun his life in that house and that was where he wanted his life to end.

When I asked Harry how he felt about Betty visiting him he said, "I enjoy seeing her but wish she'd stop feeling guilty because she didn't visit me for a while. I'm glad she's here for me. She's a stabilizing force for me now and will be during my transition to another dimension."

Betty and Harry had a talk about her guilt. She let it go so they could share happy feelings. I communicated with Harry often and he was feeling more pain. "I am only half here these days," he said. "Pain in my lungs, hard to breathe, hard to urinate, very, very tired and don't want to go on much longer. I wish to die naturally, but if there is any more pain give me relief. And I would like to die at home with my person (Betty) present." Harry reflected back to Richard his pain about the death of the marriage.

Harry's last message was, "I have been very happy, though Richard's energies are difficult to live with lately. I care about both of you and you've always cared about me." From a deeper aspect of his spirit Harry said, "I am old life and new life. I will transform and move into another dimension, changing shape and form, but my essence won't change. Learn as you watch me go through this experience. Please do not hold on to me emotionally."

Harry's pain became so great he asked to be put to sleep. Betty honored all of Harry's requests. She held Harry as he died, watching and learning as he passed from life through momentary death to life in another realm.

It's not unusual for an animal to die or leave home, or get lost, after a major event like divorce. Harry was getting old, yes; but his soul chose the time he would move into spirit form. When an animal's mission is completed, they will transform to pure spirit, or will sometimes move to another household to accomplish some other mission.

SOME ANIMALS WAVER over life and death issues, no different than we humans do.

Jonathan, a terrier, had this to say when he was hospitalized because of lethargy and loss of appetite. "I'm exhausted and scared. I feel alone. My body aches and I can't see well. All I can do is cry to let the pain out and that helps a little. A woman keeps trying to make me eat but I don't want to. I hope someone can help me feel better. I don't want to be in this strange place. I don't feel safe. Please let me out of here.

"The people here keep sticking me with sharp things and I feel like they're making me die. I don't understand it. I don't know if I want to stay in my body. It's not an easy decision and I know once I make it, it will be done. Sometimes my body and spirit feel separated, and I have trouble reconciling the different feelings I have. My spirit is sharing this with you, for the rest of me is not able to do that right now.

"I guess there's always hope. I fear if I stay in my body eventually I will feel worse even if I get better now.

"Something isn't right. Something is eating away at me inside, swollen inside. I'm confused and don't care. I do and don't. Can you help me? Let me feel your presence.

"I will wait a few days before I decide whether to stay in the body or not."

Days later Jonathan was stronger and started to eat so he went home. Within a week he was back in the hospital and sicker than ever. His people decided to have him euthanized because of his pain and what turned out to be a terminal illness.

Often when an animal is preparing to leave their body and go into the light, I see the spirit moving in and out of the body, preparing for the final separation from the physical body. I had seen this with Jonathan during the last week of his life.

MANY DOMESTIC ANIMALS I've communicated with are at times more fearful of circumstances surrounding dying than they are of the actual dying. They are frightened and don't want to die in an unfamiliar place, like a hospital. Nor in the hands of strangers, but with their human companions. Having no control over how or what their person decides to do with them can be truly terrifying to some.

Would any of us want to die in an unfamiliar place with strangers?

Most animals communicate to me that they want their people to be with them as they leave the body.

Yes, it's painful for us, but our steadfast friends have given us comfort and love through the good and bad times. How can we not be there for them?

Let us consider our animal friend's needs first and foremost as they leave this plane. I'm not minimizing the pain we feel, because it is there. But if we let the pain flow through us rather than resisting it, which creates more pain, we can move to a deeper level of inner strength and peace. Being centered allows us to be present for animal companions when they need us most. And they feel this, which automatically helps to center them and allows their essence to experience a smoother transition from body in to pure spirit.

Some animals ask to be euthanized, and some prefer to leave their body naturally. It depends on many variables, a main one being severity of pain. Age, physical condition, and response to medication are other relevant factors. If circumstances permit, let an animal choose between a natural death and euthanasia.

Is My Animal Friend in Pain?

MANY PEOPLE CALL ME to communicate with their aging animals. I love working with older animals because they can always use the support. People are often surprised when I share with them that their animals are in pain. Some people say, "Well, he's limping just a little," or "he's getting up a bit slower because he has arthritis." But people act shocked when I tell them that their animal is in pain.

This may be because we can't bear to accept that our animal friend is suffering; or it may be denial that our beloved one is getting ready to cross over into the light. Or maybe we're just not hearing what they are communicating to us. It can be challenging to get clarity about these things when we are so emotionally connected to them.

Some animals can be very stoic. It could be easy to assume that such an animal is not hurting.

Animals deal with pain in a different way than we do, but there are those who openly show their pain. It can be tricky to tell what the animal is feeling physically. This is where communication can make things clear, though you might need to ask someone else to do the communication.

Fear of Death

HUMANS' BIGGEST FEAR is death, and we wonder if we will suffer as we die. Our cultural and personal fears may be absorbed by animal companions and can cause them to become fearful about death. I communicate with animals who are fearful of death from their personality level or who don't want to leave because they feel their person still needs or wants them present. It's important to release an animal friend into the light so they can move on easily. When we struggle with the death of an animal companion we struggle with our own beliefs about death, and about mortality and immortality.

Guilt

ALMOST EVERYONE who has had an animal companion euthanized has experienced guilt. We loved our animal friend and wonder if we made the best choice. Maybe we could have done something to save them. We wonder if we had the right to end their life, and we know we're responsible for that final act.

When my cat companion, Bella, was euthanized, I wrestled with guilt. I wondered if I had her euthanized too soon. Maybe I should have given her more of a chance to regain her health. I should have had her put to sleep in a different way, a better way. There must have been something I could have done but didn't.

With time, I was able to let go of all the "shoulds" and "what ifs" and regrets. Guilt kept me tied in knots for a while, which I knew wouldn't help me or bring her back. It took me time to process my feelings.

Releasing Animal Friends

IT'S GOOD FOR US to release our animal friends into the light and love of God to help them move on. This is best for our emotional health and for the animal's soul.

One night, after Bella's departure, something happened to help me put her death into perspective.

I was curled up on my bed with my face buried in my hands, crying because I missed Bella. Suddenly, I felt Chloe jump up onto the bed. She walked over and sat directly in front of me. She pushed her face against mine and silently said, "I'm here with you. This time is sad for me, too." I looked into Chloe's eyes, hugged her and thanked her for reminding me to live in the present—and that she, too, was grieving and needed comfort. Somehow, it became easier to release Bella.

Bella's death happened as I was just learning how to telepathically communicate with animals in 1979, so I learned a great deal from walking through that experience.

Rituals

IT HELPS TO DO some kind of meaningful ritual when releasing an animal friend who has moved into the light. I lit white candles and burned incense. Then I sat down and wrote a letter to Bella telling her how she had blessed my life. I read a favorite poem, sang a song to her, prayed for a smooth transition, and cried, knowing that her spirit would still be around awhile. Releasing our animal friends into the arms of the Creator allows them to go on and do whatever is next.

Baby Gorilla

ONE EVENING, I VISITED a very sick and tiny baby gorilla who was receiving special care at a children's hospital that had agreed to treat him on an in-patient basis. When I rocked him in my arms he'd cry in pain. Telepathically he said, "I'm going to die within the next few days. There's too much pain. I'm exhausted and having trouble breathing, so much pain. I'm ready to leave my body."

We made a heart-to-heart connection and I gently balanced his chakras in a way that would offer temporary relief and help him exit his body more easily.

Three days later this brave gorilla died, leaving the doctors, nurses, and others who cared for him devastated.

Part of me wished they had just let him die when he first became ill. Another part of me had hope, and wanted him alive and well. The evening I held him in my arms, I heard his strong soul say, "My purpose here is bigger than what it seems on the surface. I am here to teach humans about the similarities and differences of other forms of life. We hurt and laugh and cry just as they do." This young gorilla lived his short life literally in the midst of hundreds of humans who cared about his welfare.

Death Is Natural

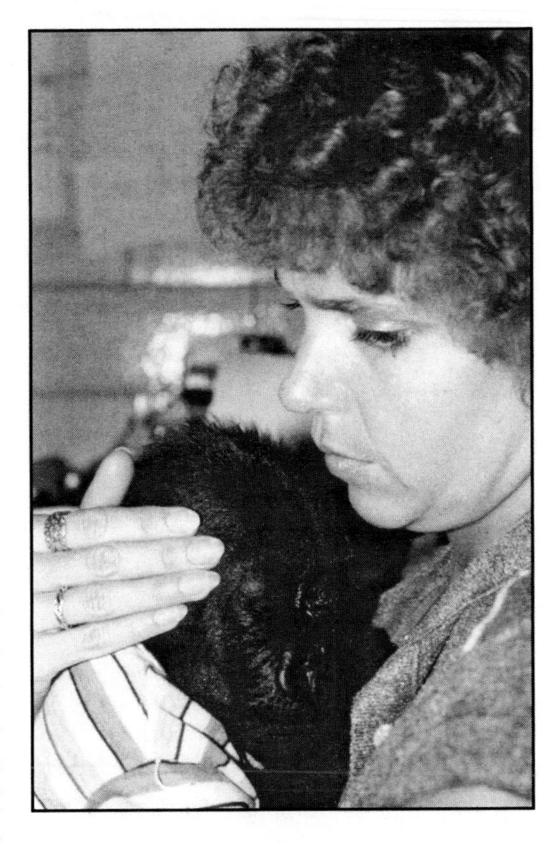

Jacquelin communicating with baby gorilla.

ANIMALS IN THE WILD live in the midst of life and death every day. There death is as natural as life. Both predator and prey play a major role in the balance of Mother Nature, and they instinctively know they are a part of her ever-changing cycles. The animals flow with rather than against her. Death is a natural phase to pass through in order to transform and move into the light, and continue living. But the domestic animal has been removed from most, if not all, natural surroundings and doesn't view or experience death in the same way. As I have mentioned, the fear that some domestic animals experience about death may stem from the personality level or they may absorb it from their person.

Ginger

GINGER, A GORDON SETTER, and her human Mary experienced a unique kind of love and commitment.

Mary wanted me to find out how much pain Ginger was in, and if she wanted to be put to sleep. Ginger was seventeen years old. She was having great difficulty with bladder control, arthritis, loss of hearing, eyesight and, appetite. Mary had a part-time job so she could take care of Ginger. Mary was helping Ginger get up and down and walk. She was also feeding her at times and carrying her upstairs at night so she could sleep by the bed as she had for many years.

Mary said,"We've learned a lot together and help balance each other. We've survived a bad marriage, a move from country to city, and an adjustment from school to work.

"Last year when I lost my job and got out of another bad relationship, that's when Ginger got hit by a car and her health has never been the same.

"I took a vacation to get away from the guy and job. A female acquaintance came to stay with Ginger. I arrived home from vacation to find Ginger lying on the front porch bleeding. When I ran into the house to ask the girl what had happened, her response was a casual, 'Oh, Ginger got hit by a car on Friday but she seemed okay.'"

The girl hadn't called a veterinarian and had left Ginger lying on the porch for almost three days. It was later discovered that Ginger's hindquarters had broken bones and torn ligaments.

When I asked Ginger about the accident, she showed me pictures as she silently spoke. "The girl wasn't nice or caring. I didn't like her and felt better outside. I was upset and was running across the street to get away from the girl. I didn't look around and got hit by a car. I was in pain after I was hit and she didn't care. The girl just continued with what she was doing. (Never have someone stay with your animal who doesn't care.)

"After that incident I never felt well, still don't. My will has been affected by never feeling well. I am waiting to die and I'm not sure how I feel about it. You ask me how I feel about death. It's okay with me for I'm very tired and have lived a full life. Not an easy one, but Mary has been a tremendous spirit in my life. I love her more than anything. She cares about me, but I don't want to be a burden to her. This is just as difficult for me as it is for her, but I don't think she's aware of this. It's embarrassing and degrading to have to be carried around and fed by her. Not to see or hear as well as when I was a pup is very hard. Growing old isn't something I think about, but when you ask me about such things, I remember and want to be puppy again. Death does not scare me. It will be a welcome relief for me and for Mary.

"I miss running and playing as I used to do. Don't want to live much longer." With this Ginger mentally showed me memories of herself running and catching a Frisbee while playing in the park surrounded by children. When I mentioned this to Mary she laughed and said that catching a Frisbee and being with the children in the park were her favorite activities.

"You ask if I'm in pain. You know I am. I feel like I can't take one more step.

"Fresh air and being on grass makes me feel better, even if I can't run anymore. I don't wish to live with the kind of pain I feel, but I'm not ready to die just yet. There are a few more experiences I want with Mary. I am beginning to say goodbye so we both get used to the idea. We are extremely close, as you know.

"I know it's been difficult for Mary to take care of me, and I appreciate all she is doing for me. I sense her sadness and pain, but if she will feel happy, I will too. She loves me deeply. In a way, I have been safe to love, and when I leave this life she will risk loving others."

Ginger communicated these messages through me to Mary: "I am thankful you treat me as an equal and not as some dumb pet as humans sometimes do. I thank you for respect, love, admiration, and the wonderful connections of understanding between us. I'm glad you are a loving human."

The only way I knew to support Mary was to listen.

One day I visited Ginger to see how she was doing and as I walked toward her, her pain was so great that it literally sent my body reeling backwards. If Ginger had been in a human body, she would have been screaming in agony. I knew any physical contact would be impossible, so I proceeded to use the Healing With Hands Technique above her body to create a soothing flow in her energy field.

As Ginger and I sat on the floor, she showed me an image of a mirror upstairs. "When I see my reflection," she said, "I feel embarrassed and ashamed. I look awful." I could sense her embarrassment and my eyes filled with tears.

From my heart I silently sent, "You are beautiful and loved."

Mary said that when she carried Ginger upstairs, she would stand in front of a mirror and talk to Ginger's reflection.

Ginger told me that, when she couldn't walk anymore, that would be the time to be put to sleep. That time came quickly, but Ginger was at peace because she had been given choices about completing her life. Mary took Ginger to the country to spend the day together before having her euthanized. Mary created a day of enjoyment and tried to give Ginger everything she desired—a day filled with green grass, blue skies, hugs, tears, painful goodbyes, and love.

I will never forget Ginger's bright, gentle soul.

Decisions

Euthanasia is a permanent decision, so both the animal and their person need time, if that's possible, to determine if it is what the animal companion really wants.

Sometimes, we ask the veterinarians to do all they can to keep our companion animals alive as long as possible. The animal may not want this, especially if they are in agony and want to be released from their body. Some want to live to a certain point in time, while others desire to die naturally despite their pain. Let us respect their choices. Some people sense intuitively when their animal friend is ready to leave this plane.

Preparing for the Journey

PEOPLE OFTEN CONTACT ME because they want to know if their companion is okay and to find out what he has to say about getting ready to cross over into the light. I like to have heart-to-heart conversations with those who are getting ready to leave the Earth plane. This gives the animal the opportunity to express any fears, conflicts, confusion, peaceful feelings, joy, or whatever else they might feel about what's happening. This also gives the person information about what their animal's wishes are concerning their death. I pass this information on to the animal's beloved person.

Some people ask me to remain attuned with their beloved animal friend as he exits the body and moves into the light.

I pray and watch as the angels and other beings of light come and lift the animal's spirit into a brilliant white light. The angels welcome the animal's soul home with open arms. I like giving this kind of support to an animal, even though it can be emotionally difficult at times. It's a gift to be able to see, through my inner eyes, the transformation happen. What an awe-inspiring sight it is to watch the angels guide the spirit home. I feel humbled and honored to be a part of this transformation process with the animals and their people.

Animals Killed on Roadways

I WORK IN A SIMILAR WAY when I see animals who have just been killed on roadways. Immediately, I attune myself with their spirit to see if they want assistance in some way, for example in understanding what has just occurred. I pray and watch the angels come and wrap them in their wings of love. The angels explain to the animal's spirit what has happened. Right after dying, some animals, especially those whose death is sudden, may be panic-stricken and dart or wander around the physical body. They may not yet know their body is dead. If they've been dead for a little while, most know what happened, but may feel lost and might have trouble finding their way into the light. Some are apprehensive about leaving their bodies behind and don't understand they can't get back into them, or take their bodies with them.

If their body is in the street, I move it onto the grass and tune into their spirit. I pray, and the animal's spirit follows the angels and higher beings of light who guide them home to their Maker.

Star

A CLOSE CAT FRIEND of mine, Star, recently died. She had been ill for several months, and knew she was going to die. Yet she wasn't sure if it was okay for her to die. Star voiced her wish to die a natural death at home.

One evening I called her person Sandy, to find out how they were doing. Sandy told me Star was going downhill.

I had been thinking about Star all day and knew I had to go see her right away. When I got there she was lying very still in her cat bed. Every breath was painful and required great effort. I spent time alone with Star to tell her how much I valued her and our friendship. I thanked her for the lessons she had taught me, and others, about spontaneity, patience, and love.

The suffering Star was going through was troubling Sandy and me. I asked Star if she wanted to be put to sleep and her response was, "I'll think about it tonight. Is it really okay for me to go?" She wanted permission to cross over into the light.

I let her know it was all right for her to leave the body whenever she was ready. I telepathically said to her, "Death is just a moment in which you transform, a split second, to leap from the body into the light."

Sandy came back into the room and the three of us sat together. Sandy and I started talking about death—how scary and nebulous it seemed because of the misconceptions our culture holds about it. We talked about our own fears, even though we both had experienced contact with those who are in the light. We agreed that when people finally let go of a dying loved one, the loved one usually dies and exits their body quickly.

Sandy and I suddenly looked at each other, then at Star. We realized our conversation had been important for Star and that she had heard every word. I knelt down and stroked Star to send her love and peace and to say goodbye.

The next morning Sandy called and said Star had died.

"In the middle of the night I heard her cry, so I held her in my arms. While I was holding her, she took her last breath and let go of this life. She died before I knew it. I could see and feel her spirit leave her body through the chest. [Animals often leave their bodies from the chest or crown chakra.] I sat in silence feeling sad. She was gone. But I felt happy, too, because she was out of pain and at peace in the light."

Sandy and I cried over the loss of a special friend who loved everyone. When I visited Sandy later that day, we could feel Star's presence around us. Star communicated she was happy to be out of her body and glad Sandy let her die at home in familiar surroundings with people she loved and who loved her.

Chloe

WHEN CHLOE, MY CAT COMPANION of twenty-two years, died of old age I was devastated. We had been together for almost half of my life, and all of her life. I embraced her and prayed as she was getting ready to cross over. I watched her spirit rise into the arms of angels who gathered around her. I was weeping. As I held her limp body she communicated, "I'm up here floating just below the ceiling, not in that body. I'm okay. Look at all the angels, the light, feel the love. Hear them singing. I'm joyful to be out of the body. No more pain. Celebrate!" And the room literally filled with light.

Even though I was grateful Chloe was out of pain and happily winging her way into the light, I was in deep in grief. Days later, she communicated from her soul, "I know you miss touching me, and I miss being touched. But both of us will be fine and we'll go on. Remember that I came into your life to help you open your heart after difficult times. I came to teach you what deeper love is. Go on in life and be open-hearted. That was my gift to you, so go on and love freely. In doing this, you honor my life."

Two months later, Etheria, my thirteen-year-old cockatiel companion, died suddenly, due to an enlarged heart. She communicated, "I wanted to be with Chloe in the light. I was tired and chose to leave my body. But both of us are around you. We're not dead, just transformed. Hear me sing."

Let us remember that death never separates us from love, and that love is the only truth.

Chapter Fourteen

Beyond Death

NOW LET'S LOOK BEYOND DEATH, where life goes on in a different way and in other dimensions. Death is like walking through a doorway. Death is a transition.

The physical body can be thought of as old clothing that we take off and leave behind as our spirit walks through death's doorway. When our spirit reaches the other side of the doorway, it's alive, conscious, and ready for a different kind of life. As one orange tiger cat put it, "Death is really no big deal. But sometimes we get very attached to our clothing."

In death, our bodies are like shadows being left behind as the spirit lifts into the light. Leaving the body behind allows a new freedom.

MANY HUMANS VIEW the body as a structure that contains the soul. But the body is created by the soul, the same way an idea exists before we manifest it into physical form. As I mentioned earlier, when I use the term "soul," it refers to the highest divine energy of who we are that creates our physical form. When I refer to "spirit," I'm talking about the life force within the body that lifts out after death, rises into the light, and rejoins with the soul.

The soul creates whatever physical form it desires for each life time in order to learn the lessons it wants to learn.

Souls who have incarnated and/or reincarnated in animal bodies are learning lessons just as we are.

NANCY CALLED ME about her cat Cammy, who insisted on hunting. He would bring trophies home and lay them on her porch. What was disconcerting to Nancy was that all the prey he brought home were headless. Cammy would bite off their heads.

Nancy wanted me to ask him to please stop beheading the chipmunks and squirrels.

When I communicated with Cammy, I immediately saw a past life in which he had been human. He had been an excellent headhunter in an ancient tribe. This behavior had been carried forward into his current lifetime.

I communicated to Cammy that he had done his work well in a previous life, but that he was now living a different life and didn't need to use those skills. I asked him to think about how it would feel if someone bit his head off.

I asked if he would be willing to consider respecting all life forms and to let Nancy know how much he appreciated her in other ways.

Nancy contacted me several months later to let me know that Cammy had not brought home any headless prey since the communication. In fact, she said that he had only brought home one gift since the communication period. It's been over a year, and he's still doing well at leaving the past lifetime in the past.

Cammy had realized he didn't have to continue the behavior from the tribal past life and let it go.

OUR CONCEPTS OF TIME AND SPACE are superficial structures we've created to live in. The way we think of time and space gives a sense of order to the physical body and plane, but we need to look beyond our clocks and physical structures. This way, we can experience other aspects and dimensions of reality and move beyond limiting views about death and life. Most of the time, we end up catching only a small glimpse of reality.

If we gaze at a pretty red rose we notice the flower, stem, thorns, and leaves. What we don't see is the root system growing beneath the soil, which is the plant's source of life. The rose couldn't exist without the roots, even though we can't see them. So, we don't see the "whole" but just a part of the plant's being.

We tend to focus on the outward appearance of someone or something, like the rose, rather than looking into the essence, or root system. This is why many think of death as the final curtain.

After an Animal Crosses Over

WHEN SPIRIT LEAVES the body and crosses over into the light, it re-joins with its soul. Whatever thoughts it thinks become an immediate reality. This is because the material body no longer inhibits the flow of energy in any way. Yet those who have discarded the body can still feel constricted if they create and surround themselves with limiting thoughts. Usually after gaining experience, they learn how to release old ideas and patterns they used while in the body. This tends to happen more with humans than with animals.

I have found that animals I communicate with in other dimensions seem to rapidly attune themselves to their new environment with assistance from the angels and loved ones who are in the light, as well as other beings of light whose mission it is to help new arrivals adjust.

When people call me to communicate with their beloved animal friends only days after they have crossed over, I usually see their animal companion wrapped in a beautiful cocoon of light and vibrant colors. The animal is surrounded by angels and other beings of light. These beings are helping to heal the animal's etheric body (aura) and whatever else needs to be healed. If an animal was very ill, she may remain in the cocoon of light for a longer period.

Since souls are multidimensional, an animal's soul can be healing in the cocoon of light while a part of her spirit is still walking beside us, sleeping next to us, or pawing litter, while the same soul is living many other lives simultaneously in other bodies in various dimensions, galaxies, and realities. All souls are vast and more complex than we can ever imagine.

When the soul crosses over, the beings of light assist the soul in reviewing the life they've just experienced on Earth.

PRAYERS AND MEDITATIONS help our animal friends to make a smoother transition. It's a good idea to continue praying or doing meditations for them for a while after they've crossed over. These prayers are heard and assist the soul in continuing its journey.

Letting Go of Influences

EVEN THOUGH DOMESTIC ANIMALS lived in our physical structures and were influenced by our ego struggles, they aren't stuck in or attached to ego structures as humans are. Spirits that were human sometimes take more time to release themselves from ego concerns because they think of the ego as part of their true identity, though it's not. But when they listen to inner wisdom, they let go of identifying with the ego. Animals let go of our influence shortly after leaving their body. Yet they, too, have to deal with their own patterns and perceptions and process the life they have just lived on Earth.

Messages

AN ANIMAL'S SPIRIT usually uses their most recent personality to communicate through, probably to be recognized by their person. The soul remembers various personality patterns from different lifetimes and may talk about the lessons being learned.

Beings that lived in animal form communicate all kinds of messages to me after leaving their bodies. Some convey why they lived in particular circumstances or may mention qualities they reflected to their people. Others silently tell about why they died or why they chose the particular species and body form they did in life. A number of animals describe their experiences about the different dimensions and offer insight into spiritual ties they've had, and have, with their person through many lifetimes.

A WOMAN'S COMPANION DOG Lucky was euthanized because of a terminal illness. She wanted to know what he wished to communicate from his spirit.

"I know what you did was one of the hardest things you've ever had to do. My message is one of love, and my hope is you'll release the guilt about the way my life ended. I felt joyful about leaving my body because I was in pain. Thank you for comforting me as my life ended.

"I am enjoying zooming through walls. There is no heat or coldness where I am.

"Our relationship was true friendship rather than one of ownership or control. There was a give and take that doesn't often happen between an animal and a human. Thanks."

DELPHI, A SIAMESE CAT had this to say after being in the light for about five months: "It has been hard to let go of everyone and everything I loved. I do miss eating, my feeling senses, your touch, and my favorite couch cushion. I go in and out of the house whenever I please and walk through the flower beds outside."

Delphi telepathically showed and told me she missed a girl who she was especially fond of. The cat's person said it was her older daughter.

Sally and her family were vacationing in Oregon and while driving spotted a black cat running along the side of the road. She stopped the car, picked him up, plopped him on the seat, and drove home to Seattle.

After a few years, she and her family decided to live where they had vacationed in Oregon. Of course, Max, the cat, moved with them.

The move and change of lifestyle added more tension to an already stressful situation that stemmed from marital problems. It took its toll on everyone, including Max.

They were in Oregon barely six months when they decided to go on vacation for two weeks. Before leaving, they dropped Max off at the veterinarian for minor surgery.

The stress of the surgery triggered a leukemia virus from a dormant to active stage. The day after coming home Sally had Max put to sleep.

Sally wanted to know about his death and anything else Max wanted to communicate.

"I tried to hold my ground," he said, "but I slipped into the stress everyone was feeling. Angry feelings were passed around the house and so I wanted to be outside more often because of all the strain. Not enough outlets for the tension everyone held within. So much sadness, tears, and pain from Sally.

"I was upset because my people weren't here when I had surgery. I wondered if everyone left for good. I was confused in unfamiliar surroundings. My system couldn't handle it all.

"You [Sally] need to take care of yourself so the stress doesn't attack your body. Find some outlets.

"When you found me it was hard for me to leave the area. I was so glad to come back to where I was born before dying. I am enjoying roaming in the grass and jumping after bugs, but I get confused and forlorn. I feel lost at times and don't understand why no one hears or pays attention to me. It has been a hard break for me." Max was still accepting that he had crossed over and wasn't in his body.

As with Max, it can take an animal time to accept and feel attuned as they adjust to being in the light.

Connections

After an animal companion dies, it may be helpful to look at what he mirrored to us about ourselves and to ask: What was I like and what was going on in my life when I got this friend? How have I changed since that time? Does the timing of my animal's death have significant meaning?

Many people whose animals I communicate with see connections between important changes or events in their lives and the timing of their friend's death.

Animals can cross over as relationships end, when people move, or shortly before or after a family member moves into the light. Sometimes the animal is simply ready to move into another dimension.

As I have mentioned, when animals communicate, their personality traits as well as spiritual insight and universal wisdom flow through them. The same is true after the animal has shed its body.

Tandy, Mustard, and Other Communications

ANDREA'S TWO CAT COMPANIONS died within seven months of each other. "I feel them jumping up and down on my bed at night," she said. "Are they really around the house and do they hear me talk to them? What are they experiencing?"

Tandy silently said, "Yes, I'm around the house. I visit early in the morning while you're in bed and when you retire. Mustard is there, too. I realize you don't see me, but I certainly know you feel me. And I still enjoy being in the kitchen.

"Yes, I hear what you say to me. I understand your vibration that goes far beyond words people mutter.

"I enjoy being in the light. My body was very tired when I left it. I feel more alive now.

"I like being around you even though I'm not in the body anymore. I come and go. It's easy to travel wherever I wish without the body. I'm happy and free, healing.

"Thank you for your love. I feel lucky to have been with you while in the body. In a previous life I had to work very hard for my meals, catching mice for my master. The life with you in a warm home was complete and restful.

"You can know what I say if you listen with your heart. Trust what you hear, it's not your imagination."

When I asked Mustard to communicate messages for her human, she said, "Tandy and I are together but we go our own ways in order to learn whatever we wish to learn.

"I have to tell you, I was so upset when Tandy left her body that I decided to leave too. I mourned for her for months and did not want to go on even though you were loving. You were so sad, too.

"I never felt sure about myself, unlike Tandy. I am now understanding myself. It was hard for me to adjust to some circumstances while in the body and still is even without the body.

"I, like Tandy, am around and I am often at the foot of your bed. Sometimes I whisper colors of wisdom into your ear in the middle of the night or at early dawn. I know you hear me within yourself.

"I worried quite a bit while in the body and have learned to let go of that pattern. Some of the worrying came from thoughts in the environment and from each other. I miss physical touch and sitting on soft things.

"I'm learning a lot and I am happier out of the body. I feel freer and released from some of my own struggles about having existed in a small body. But that was part of what I needed to experience.

"Thank you for sharing your life with me.

"Something souls who were human learn when they come into this other side of life is that what was important was not the bodily form, but the expression of each being's soul. The love."

I was deeply moved by the communications from these two wise, loving felines.

A WOMAN CALLED ME FROM TEXAS to communicate with her collie, Thomas, who had just crossed over into the light. Thomas wanted me to tell his person that he would let her know that he was alive and well within a day. She called me the next evening saying that when she got home from work that a photograph of Thomas, which was sitting on the mantle, was lying on the floor.

Another woman's cat whom I had communicated with about moving into the light made a dramatic exit. As the veterinarian was euthanizing her, her spirit shot out of her body and through a light catcher of a dolphin hanging on the window, which fell and shattered.

Bill's cat told me he was tired and sick and wanted to go rest in the light. Not long after he died, Bill heard wings flapping from behind a window shade, at the place where his cat used to sleep on a chair. He pulled up the shade and there was a yellow and black butterfly—from where? We both knew this was a visitation.

After Chloe died, I would hear her pawing the litter and feel her padding her way across my bed many nights. My sheets moved with her every step and pounce.

Marlene called to tell me that a stray dog had come to her door the morning after her dog Brad had crossed over. She opened the door and the dog ran in and sat in the same place Brad used to sit. Then the dog went into another room and came back to Marlene, carrying the only toy that she had kept of Brad's. She had thrown all the others away.

They played for a while and then the dog pawed at the door to leave.

Brad communicated to me that he had borrowed the dog's body to play with Marlene one more time before more fully moving into the light.

These are not uncommon occurrences after an animal moves into the light. They want their people to know they're alive and well. Animals will also come in dreams. Chloe still visits me in my dreams and it is always wonderful to spend time with her.

A Cat Who Didn't Want to Let Go

A FRIEND CALLED ME FROM CALIFORNIA because her cat companion James had disappeared into a canyon, which was actually her backyard. (I had done a few consults with her animal companions, including James, helping with a move from Ohio to California.) I told her he was alive but injured and couldn't come home. She searched without results. We talked a few days later and I knew he was now in spirit form, but not in the light.

I communicated with James and he told me he didn't want to be out of the body and had been trying to get back in. I asked his guardian angels to help him understand it wasn't going to work. I could see clairvoyantly that when he had first left his body, he ignored the light helpers and ended up wandering around the canyon in spirit. But even after understanding this, he was still stuck and couldn't move on. So I asked Spirit for understanding and like a flash of light, his cat brother Charlie yowled at me telepathically: "I'm not letting him go." I spent time helping Charlie understand that the most loving act would be to release James into the angels' arms. He finally agreed with deep sadness to let go. I felt my heart open as Charlie released James and then everything shifted.

James accepted being in spirit form and was happy he had found his way into the light.

I told Charlie if he opened his third eye and heart he'd now be able to see James's spirit and know that he was just fine, that they could chat any time. Charlie sighed and smiled.

Communicating with Animals in Spirit

COMMUNICATING WITH ANIMALS in other dimensions is as natural as communicating with animals who are physically here with us. You follow the same steps. You're communicating with the essence of the animals that lives on. But to do this, it's important to move beyond any limiting beliefs about death, time, space, and reality. Just let your intuition guide you beyond body and mind. The animals will show you the way.

Reincarnation

MANY ANIMALS, like Tandy, mention other lifetimes. My thoughts about other lifetimes have emerged from my experiences of communicating with souls that have lived in both human and nonhuman form.

I personally have many memories of previous lives. As I was recalling one past lifetime in China, I wrote down a series of letters or symbols in a column. I asked a friend to show them to an ancient language professor at a university. He was taken aback and said that every symbol was from a particular ancient dialect in China. After this experience, I knew that past lives were real. And no, I never studied Chinese.

The thought of other lifetimes might not feel comfortable to the mind, but that's because the idea and experience is somewhat foreign to Western culture.

The process of living many lives encompasses various dimensions and realities, which gives our souls a more balanced glimpse of the whole. We experience a variety of lifetimes and forms to learn about the spiritual, physical, and other states of being that exist. This offers our souls the opportunity to be compassionate and loving toward others.

Soul energy creates physical form, and when the form dies, spirit returns to soul again. The soul can create as many forms as it desires, physical as well as etheric, and is living in many of these forms and alternative realities simultaneously.

Reincarnation is a circle of beginnings and completions, of life and death. Cycles are natural, like the circling of seasons, the moon's waxing and waning, and the rhythm of the tides. We may become frightened because we can't see or touch these unseen realities, but by using inner eyes, ears, and senses we can perceive many of these other dimensions and realities.

All beings reflect and express different aspects of the Creator, like a multifaceted crystal. Using the concept of the wheel I discussed earlier, no being is higher or lower. A fly's life has purpose, just as a human's does.

Evolution of Soul

Evolution is not linear. The wheel is always turning like the planets. Moving around on this cosmic wheel allows souls to experience each others' perspectives, whether it be on Earth or in other realities, dimensions, galaxies, or Universes.

This gives everyone the opportunity to "know" each others' experience, to feel the interconnectedness, to understand that we are all one.

Some people believe that "lowly" forms in the animal kingdom remain within their species when they are born again into the physical form. For example, once a cat, always a cat. I have not found this to be true. Others believe that animals don't have individual souls and that when they die they are absorbed back into their collective species consciousness level. There are species consciousness levels, which we are all a part of, but animals do have individual souls beyond the species level, just as we do.

We create barriers between humans and other beings by saying other life forms don't have the gift of eternal life, or have it to a much lesser degree. I am a dog, cat, bird, tree, and human. The outer form is different, but soul is soul. We are all one. It's a unity of spirit that shows us the Creator's wholeness.

I know a wise and gifted dog educator who says, "I know beyond a shadow of a doubt that I've been a dog before. I know them inside and out." And I had picked up that he had been a dog in a past life. The soul aspect communicates from beyond familiar personality patterns. This spark has limitless depths of great universal wisdom, insight, and joy. I doubt if any of us will ever understand or be able to explain all the complex connections that make up the whole picture of many and varied realities. Yet, I am the "whole" as well as a portion of the "whole," as is every living form.

Past Life Messages

A delightful Panamanian parrot named Shirley shared a couple of lifetimes that involved her present human companion, Larry.

One life she described was as a scarlet macaw in South America. Larry was a young Indian boy who helped to heal her broken wing. Through the years, they grew very close and telepathically communicated with one another. As the boy became a man, he had a wife who gave him three children. The macaw felt displaced because of difficult changes and circumstances in that life. Later on, the macaw was broken-hearted because she outlived her human friend.

In another life, Shirley was Larry's human daughter. She lived in Africa with her father, who studied plant life. Larry's wife died from a fever when the daughter was three. Later the daughter went to England, became a nurse, and married. She and her husband returned to her father's home after many years. Then her father died and she and her husband buried him in Africa.

In her present existence, Shirley conveyed how important it is to be with Larry because of such strong soul ties. I could feel this intimate link between them. They have both chosen to be together again in this life to continue their experience.

Shirley and Larry live in the city this time round, which is quite a change of scenery. I know it's a very close connection for Shirley since she is choosing to live in a large city in parrot clothing. She may outlive Larry again since parrots live about sixty years in captivity.

One time Shirley got out of the apartment and was flying around Chicago. Larry ran a lost-and-found ad offering a reward for her return. When she was safely returned, Larry's response was, "I knew she and I were destined to be together. It must be divine intervention when an animal, especially a bird, gets lost in a giant city with millions of people and is found and returned."

Shirley is a colorful character and I had great fun conversing with her.

WHILE AT A ZOO one day, I felt an unusually strong heart-to-heart connection with a gorilla. She had been caught in the wild. I asked if she'd like to chat. She silently voiced how she enjoyed being outside in the air and on green grass, especially after having been contained inside a building, in a cage at another zoo.

After getting better acquainted, she shared some past-life experiences with me. "I have been a gorilla many times, but not always. I was a man who studied and lived with gorillas. Wanting to totally understand what they felt and how they perceived their world, I chose to be a gorilla. I am learning a tremendous amount and will come back again as a human to verbally teach humans about gorillas' experience.

"Because I am in captivity, I am learning about gorillas while teaching humans about gorillas."

CHARLIE IS A POODLE who communicated that one reason he and his person Ted were together again was to learn from each other about similar personality patterns. I could clearly see similarities being mirrored between them.

"We vibrate to the same tone, light, and rhythm," said Charlie. "To try and put this into words limits what it is. Feel it and you'll understand. Get the idea?"

Charlie went on to say to Ted, "Let's share our time together in understanding. You as human and me as dog in this life can know a new kind of closeness that we agreed to share before being born in these bodies. It's an advantage at times to be in an animal body, other than human, to understand relationships. I hope we connect in deeper ways than we have in some other lives. Our past lives number many. It's important to know we teach and learn from each other as equals."

Charlie's soul communicated to my spirit in a way that was more profound than any words, thoughts, or images. This kind of wisdom comes from the limitless cosmic depths that flow through all beings.

DENNY CALLED ME to find out about a Doberman pup, Astor, he had adopted six months ago. First, Denny explained that his beloved Doberman Starburst had died ten months ago. Astor came into his life through a series of synchronistic events. (Many people and animals tell me that they are brought together through synchronistic happenings.) Denny told me that Astor had some very specific mannerisms that Starburst had exhibited throughout his life. He felt the mannerisms went beyond the explanation of breed.

When I communicated with Astor, it was clear that a bit of Starburst's soul had reincarnated in with Astor. So there is a "mix of spirits" going on. Astor's personality and spirit are present; Starburst is also present—but not the dominant spirit.

I encouraged Denny to treat Astor as Astor, and not as Starburst. But also, to recognize, acknowledge, and enjoy the mannerisms brought in from Starburst.

Is My Animal Coming Back to Me?

I RECEIVE NUMEROUS CALLS from people wanting to know if their beloved animal companion is going to come back to them.

Each soul decides if it will reincarnate to the same person they have just lived with or not. When an animal first crosses over, the soul will often communicate to me that it has not yet been decided if it is coming back to the same person. The soul will indicate that it's not yet clear about when, where, or in what form it will choose to reincarnate.

In this instance, I suggest to the person that they call me back in three to four months when things are more settled. When people call me back, the soul has usually determined what its plans are. But sometimes as soon as an animal crosses over, the soul will tell me when it is going to reincarnate and what he or she will look like physically.

SUE CALLED AND WANTED ME to communicate with her cat Ming who had transitioned into the light a few nights before. Ming said, "I'll be back in six months and this time I'll be taking on the body of a little dog. Tell my person she'll find me in a place she wouldn't ordinarily go, and that I'll have a white star on my forehead. She'll know me when she looks into my eyes. We still have lessons to learn from various lives we've shared."

Sue doesn't usually go into pet stores. But six months later she happened to swing into one and was looking around, and there was a little dog with a white star on her forehead. Sue called me and said, "When I looked into her eyes, I knew it was Ming."

I hear many stories like this from people about their companion animals who reincarnate back to them. This typically happens when an animal's mission hadn't been completed, or when there are further lessons for everyone to learn from one another.

Will My Animals Greet Me?

PEOPLE CALL ME AND ASK if the animal companions they have known throughout their lives will be there to greet them when they cross over. The answer is yes. People are relieved to hear this, because many have been told by psychics, religious figures, and others that animals do not have souls and will not be in heaven.

One woman called me crying because a psychic had told her that animals go to one place in heaven and that humans go to another place in heaven. I told her that what I experience when communicating with animals, as well as with humans on the other side, is that they are all in heaven, or in the light. I have communicated with countless spirits of those who had been human, animal, or other forms. I see the light workers and other angelic beings who are working and living in the light.

Soul is soul, so all of us ascend into the same light from which we were created. Let us remember that we humans are animals, too. Whenever any being crosses over, regardless of what physical form they may have inhabited, they are there to greet and guide us with open arms.

Karl

ANNETTE WAS ON TRANQUILIZERS when she called and said, "I want to see you as soon as possible." Her cat, Karl, had died a week before from a stroke while having his teeth cleaned.

Karl communicated these messages to me for his person. "My stay with you was the best part of my life. You see, I was learning to trust humans again. Some experiences were good, some not good, but I could always count on you.

"My body was aching and I hurt in my bones. I decided to leave the body now so I wouldn't have to suffer in a different way later on.

"We have experienced a number of close lifetimes together. I was a lioness and you were my cub. We lived in the same pride until you were hunted down by humans. I missed you and we both welcomed being together again to learn about ourselves and each other.

"Because my death was so sudden, it was a big shock. I didn't know I had left my body for several days. When I'd walk up to you and you didn't respond to me, I knew. It isn't easy for me to be out of the body and separated from you in this way. I cry. I know you cry. I whisper thoughts into your ears at night and dawn. I will be around for a while and will then move on to different experiences.

"You certainly haven't had an easy road to walk. It's time for you to love and nurture yourself. In some ways, I gave you what you couldn't give yourself. But now you're ready to do this. Follow your heart's desire.

"Remember my bright eyes, for this will help us to connect. If you think a thought to me I will hear. Listen for my thoughts. I may come to you through images and feelings so relax and trust them.

"I send bushels of love. I feel scared and confused at times so please send me love and light. Light that's like the sun I always loved so much. I am glad to be free of the body and yet feel sad.

"Just as trees bear fruit, we too will spring forth again bearing fruit. We will be together again.

"I leave you with the image of a multi-faceted diamond which reflects the light in all its aspects."

As I spoke this last sentence about the diamond, Annette started sobbing and didn't stop for a long time. Then she said, "All this is incredible. I have been through hard times in my life and am just learning to love and think about what my heart's desires are. And Karl did love the sun more than my other animals. He and I often gazed into each other's eyes, and he had unusually bright eyes.

"But his amazing message about the diamond pierced my heart. No one in the world knew about the diamond. You see, before I buried Karl I laid him in a wooden box and put one of my diamond earrings between his paws."

She and I both sat and sobbed. His communication was an extremely beautiful, intimate gift for Annette.

I find transmitting messages like Karl's helps grieving people through difficult times. To know life goes on gives us a different perspective, one that allows us to more easily accept death, even though it means the physical loss of a companion. Knowing that they are alive and well, we can more easily put our grief to rest.

The messages I transmitted from Karl to Annette helped her to see a light of hope in the midst of dark grief. She was sad because she missed him and ecstatic because now she knew he was alive. Annette knew how he felt about her and all that had happened.

Chapter Fifteen

Heart-to-Heart Connections

HEART-TO-HEART COMMUNICATION with animals is an intimate exchange that allows us to be in touch with ourselves and an animal. It gives our relationships more depth and meaning. It is a way of being, not just something to do with an animal friend once a month or just when we want to. Sometimes, when my schedule becomes busy and I don't communicate with my animal companions for a couple days, I miss the closer, deeper communication.

Heart-to-heart communication between human and animal enhances the relationship overall. There is more openness, which allows love to flow more freely on all levels.

Having the attitude that all life is basically equal—and that, therefore, we do not own other beings—helps to form clear and open channels of communication. Being childlike allows the experience of communication to simply happen with ease.

Using nonverbal language with our animal friends helps us to heal any connections that have been broken. This, in turn, heals everyone.

My hope is for humans to allow all species to live a natural life and to fulfill their purpose, not just survive. Let us show animals the kind of compassion that they so freely give us.

Animals and other life forms are helping to raise our awareness about life and love. They are our teachers and healers. Mutual healing can take place between humans and animals. All species are part of the ever-turning wheel that continues to raise the consciousness of all life forms.

This awareness is a continuous dance of every cell, body, soul, and species in the Universe and beyond. The animals know that humans need love and compassion and they continue to teach and heal us.

The spiritual beings that exist within domestic animal forms have chosen their form for many reasons. One reason is to teach us about and encourage the higher qualities they mirror to us, such as unconditional love, cooperation, spontaneity, play, and giving. All beings—the four-legged, winged, or crawlers—have something to teach us that we can apply in practical ways to our lives.

This is not to say that animals are better than we are, only that there is much to learn from them. And just as humans assist animals, many animals assist humans. Each learning situation is a unique one between each animal and human.

Animals are learning about themselves and other life forms while here on Earth. Some animals tell me they are here to learn to trust particular people or humans in general. This is especially true if they have been through difficult experiences with humans in other lifetimes. The animals continue to love us, even though we humans abused a sacred trust that once existed among all species.

I am not belittling our species, but merely want us to recognize how we have acted in the past and that we have great potential to choose to promote and actualize goodwill among all species.

A step forward would be for us to allow animals to be who they are and stop trying to make them human-like. And even though animal friends reflect various attitudes and energies to us, it is important to look beyond those reflections, as with the form, in order to see their true souls. The ancient art of communicating silently with our animal companions and other species gives us the opportunity to reconnect with them, ourselves, our basic roots in Nature, and ultimately, with the Creator. By returning to our inner senses—our spiritual self—we experience universal love and truth. We can then remember and experience our ties with the Earth, animals, sun, moon, stars, other galaxies, and beyond. None of this can come from intellect, but from connecting with our intuition and divinity.

ALTHOUGH I HAVE CHOSEN to concentrate on heart-to-heart communication between humans and animals, this same connection is also fun and fulfilling to experience with rocks, soil, trees, streams, or any other life forms. The life force flows through each one. You can communicate with any life form in the way you would an animal. I would suggest, in communicating with any form in Nature, to imagine yourself in a bubble of white light before you begin. There are some energies in Nature that are elemental and too different for humans to connect with in a direct way. Be wise and trust your intuition.

OUR SEPARATION FROM NATURE and intuition is unnatural. Heart-to-heart or intuitive communication is natural. We've got it backward in our society. Those who consider nonhuman beings as close friends are thought of as being "off." Yet animal companions can be more honest and trustworthy than many humans.

SINCERE LOVE AND RESPECT for animals and other life forms provides a solid foundation from which to communicate silently with animals. The love we send to one animal continues to flow into and effect that particular species' consciousness level. This gives us the opportunity to help heal many species, the Earth, and ourselves. The following experience shows how this can happen.

RECENTLY I GAVE A TALK at the Midwest Ohio Veterinary Conference. Several days later a woman, Helen, called to tell me how much she had learned from my talk about respecting all life forms. Helen said, "I usually kill spiders because I'm afraid of them. The day after I heard your talk there was a spider in my bathroom. When I saw it, I screamed. Then I thought of your talk. I calmed myself and sent the spider thoughts of respect. I told him I was going to put him in a cup and carry him outside, which I did. I can no longer kill spiders. This is a major transformation and healing for me."

Helen's story touched me deeply. She had chosen to move beyond old limiting thoughts about spiders and to view them as valuable beings. She walked through her fear and put her new way of thinking about spiders into action. Wow!

ANIMALS HAVE BEEN TRYING to get our attention since we separated from Nature.

Nonverbal communication enables us to better understand and know our animal companions, which allows both the human and nonhuman to work with their personality patterns and spiritual issues.

There is tremendous joy, love, and openness in communicating with animals. The miracle is that all of us can, once again, experience the silent language of the heart with all living forms. I have heard countless animals ask us to "Please listen."

Chapter Sixteen

Evolutionary and Planetary Changes for All Life Forms

Energetic shifts are happening around the globe, in our solar system, and in other solar systems as well. Natural cycles are always taking place. This has been happening since the Earth came into being and will continue. And even though we can't possibly know all the changes the Earth and her inhabitants have been through since her birth; we certainly are in the midst of some major shifts today. These changes seem to be accelerating and are affecting all living forms in significant ways. It appears that we are moving into the next stage of our evolutionary process. I am referring to these ongoing energy and Earth changes that we are experiencing in this age as a "transition" or "shift." This simply gives a framework in which to talk about these alterations and how they are potentially playing a key role in the further development of living forms. Some readers may resonate with this material and some may not, and that's fine. I just ask that you be open to what I have been experiencing along with numerous others around the world.

People often ask me if the animals and other life forms are involved with the transition. Yes. In fact, they are a very important part of this process. Animals open us to love, which helps us remember who we truly are beyond the various masks we wear in our daily lives.

The Earth and every species are growing spiritually. We are helping one another. The creative force is always expanding through rebirth, so this evolution process makes sense. The Earth is a spiritual being with soul. She has heart. Beings from various realms, dimensions, and universes are assisting her, us, and all other life forms. She is in the midst of her own spiritual evolution and we cannot separate ourselves from her journey. The Earth and her residents are a multispecies network of complex interconnections. Many dimensions of consciousness are opening as the Earth is transforming. She is vibrating with higher frequencies, and is therefore letting go of the old densities (patterns of lower vibrations created from negative thoughts and actions) that have accumulated through time. Humankind is moving through the same process of letting go of the old. By raising our consciousness in remembering that, soul to soul, we are all connected, we help the Earth, ourselves, and all others.

THE ELECTROMAGNETIC WAVES from the sun and outer space are altering Mother Earth's magnetic fields. Part of the reason this is happening is because the ozone layer appears to be weakening. Some scientists have suggested that the Earth's geomagnetic field may also be weakening. All this, along with other energetic changes, is opening doors for higher frequencies to enter the Earth's atmosphere, as well as the Earth herself. Also, the magnetic poles are shifting. Airports around the world have had to modify the magnetic error corrections for north in regard to their airport maps so they can continue using automatic instruments. Birds are migrating to different locations due to these alterations.

The magnetic poles are shifting with our sun. There has been a higher level of solar activity, which is affecting the Earth's geomagnetic fields, weather patterns, and all living forms in one way or another. The sun's activity affects our entire solar system.

Some researchers have recently stated that more whale strandings occur when there are surges of solar activity. They say the solar flares might disrupt whales' internal compasses. This is because changes in levels of solar radiation have a big effect on the Earth's magnetic field. We know solar flares can cause problems with power grids and affect communications on Earth. This affects the interaction of energies with our sun, moon, and Earth. How can we not be affected by these shifts in vibration?

These new energies are also opening more doors interdimensionally, which allows additional light to pour over the Earth. Similar transformations are going on within our solar system, as well as within other solar systems. Beings in other worlds are experiencing these shifts too. All living forms, together, are ushering in the dawning of a new age. Remember, we are all members of the cosmic community—an interplanetary family.

By the way, not all beings, including animals, that reside on Earth have Earth origin. Their souls' origins are with other planets, stars, solar systems, dimensions, and Universes. Earth is not the only planet that is teeming with life.

Becoming More Conscious

THE ELECTROMAGNETIC AND COSMIC RAYS reaching into the Earth's atmosphere are causing shifts around us, as well as within our own physical and energy bodies. These changes can cause imbalances in the Earth's aura, our auras, and the auras of other beings; but we are being given the opportunity to rebalance ourselves in positive ways. The new energies pouring in are breaking up the Earth's karmic patterns, as well as our own karmic patterns—individually and as a species. Our souls are letting go of baggage from many lifetimes. This is a purification process. It is time for us to become more aware of our inner light so we can personally and as a race manifest more love and light. We are like diamonds in the process of being refined. This can be challenging, yet all that is happening is helping us to become more conscious and to unfold spiritually in wonderful ways.

As we progress, living forms will shift away from three-dimensional reality, duality, and fear, and into deeper dimensions of love and light. We have the opportunity to see through the illusion that we are separate from each other and to remember the truth that we are all one. It is this awakening in consciousness, individually and then collectively, that is bringing about a paradigm shift.

All of life is learning how to adapt to these new vibrations as we continue to be showered with higher frequencies of light and love.

We are learning about being heart rather than letting mind and ego run our lives. We are being asked to respect and love the divinity within. The Creator's spirit within us is who we truly are and will be after our bodies are gone. If we travel into the inner sacred space or dimensions of heart, this is where we come to know the Divine, ourselves, each other, and truth. As we remember how to love unconditionally from our inner divinity, this raises the frequencies for all. It also helps us to become aligned with the Creator and all of creation so we can fulfill our potential and purpose here on Earth.

As more light continues to flood the Earth, our light bodies, souls, and higher selves are slowly integrating with our physical bodies. Every being is doing this at whatever pace his or her soul chooses. It is a marriage of spirit and matter. We will eventually experience transmutation on the DNA and cellular level as we integrate all aspects of ourselves. You could say that we are being rewired.

As the Earth and other living forms integrate the deeper dimensions of love and light, we will have the chance to live in the physical world in a loving and peaceful way. As we accept more light and love, miracles will become the norm. The Earth is not going to end, but it is transforming into a new Earth. These shifts are moving us beyond limiting views of what many have thought reality is. Of course, the mind has trouble trying to grasp all this. The ego doesn't want to let go of familiar structures, even though they are illusions, so it fights change. It's best if we can surrender to the changes. Old structures humans have created within institutions of religion, politics, economics and many others will continue to crumble. To many this feels like the end of the world, but by releasing the old we can create a better world.

It also seems that time is being altered. People tell me that they are experiencing time differently. Some days it seems to speed up and other days or weeks it seems to slow down. The length of our day is actually shorter since the earthquake and tsunami in Eastern Asia. (Even though it was only 2.68 microseconds, how could that not have an effect?)

As we move through these transitions, we are in the process of moving into living in every moment. Time is only an arbitrary structure we created to give order to this physical world.

The higher frequencies being introduced now are ultimately helping us to understand that we are more powerful beings than we think we are. Yet at a deeper level, we already know this to be true. We are multidimensional beings, living and learning lessons in many dimensions and realities simultaneously. Our souls are gradually integrating the various aspects of ourselves from other realms. As we awaken from our sleep, we are expanding and realizing what wonderful beacons of light and love we are. We are moving back/forward to the Garden of Eden, symbolically, or returning to love and peace, when all beings knew and expressed only love and communicated silently with one another—when we knew that we are all one. This was before ego led us astray. The animals have retained their intuition. Our intuition for the most part has been shoved aside by ego. Yet now we are reconnecting with our natural intuitive abilities in bigger ways.

With more light showering the Earth, our chakra systems are being activated and are expanding. Our chakras (energy system of spinning wheels of light in the aura and etheric body that help sustain our physical, mental, emotional, and spiritual balance) and those of the animals, other life forms, and the Earth are changing vibrationally. Chakras that have been dormant for a very long time are now opening. The development of our chakra system is key in terms of evolving more fully. Remember that we are energy. Soul creates whatever body it desires in which to have an experience. These changes in the chakra system will support us in actualizing our intuitive skills, as well as helping us to fulfill our multidimensional soul's purpose. This connects us in a positive, dynamic way to our cosmic self as well as the cosmos. Knowledge about the cosmos that has been stored in the subconscious is now becoming conscious for many people around the globe.

Animals, along with other living forms, are our teachers and guides. They are assisting humankind with waking up.

As we travel toward the light and love within ourselves, it can be challenging. These higher vibrations are assisting us in releasing and forgiving old wounds so all can heal, and in order for us to learn whatever lessons we need to learn. We are being asked to open our hearts, to love ourselves and others, whether that other being is a cat, dog, fly or a being from another galaxy. The animals and other life forms are leading us into our hearts to help heal us and the Earth. Let us remember to celebrate the beauty on Earth.

As the old ego-centered energies continue to be cleared, let us welcome in the higher, deeper love vibration; let us support and be compassionate with each other. The mind cannot possibly comprehend all these shifts, but the soul does. Therefore, it's important to simply flow with the changes and not try to analyze everything. As these shifts take place, one might feel as if one foot is planted in this world while the other foot is loose and fancy free in other realms. Those who are very sensitive to energy have told me this is what it feels like for them. I have experienced these sensations myself. As we evolve, we will become more in tune with the new chakra system that is unfolding and being refined.

Many people have been asking me what is going on because they are feeling these shifts around as well as within themselves. They say the vibrations feel completely different from what they have experienced before.

SINCE I TEND to be very sensitive to energies, I have found myself swimming in and out of various dimensions spontaneously countless times. At first it was disorienting and I wasn't sure what was going on, but the angels and other beings of light helped me understand that it was due to the increase of changes going on around the Earth as well as within me.

I have had a number of experiences of moving into another dimension while standing within five feet of other people. When this has occurred, the people could not see or hear me. A couple of times, a friend who was standing next to me found herself in this other dimension with me. In an effort to convince her of this, I began to sing loudly and wave my arms wildly to get the other people's attention. She then did the same. We laughed, we danced. There was no recognition or response from the people who were standing around us in a quiet business office. I'm always ecstatic to have a witness when such things happen. I'm sure you can understand why.

The many dimensions I have experienced and continue to experience are like being in a kaleidoscope of shifting shapes and brilliant colors. I have met unique, wonderful beings who exist in other realms and worlds. Some are strictly etheric, while others can materialize and dematerialize at will.

As we expand our way of thinking and being we will know that all things are possible. Everyone has the ability to explore other dimensions and Universes. Even though we are rooted to the Earth by our bodies, we can soar beyond time and be anywhere we desire in a flash. But first we must believe we can.

The Animals and Other Life Forms Speak

ANIMALS CONTINUE TO COMMUNICATE messages to me about the changes that are going on. The following messages from the animals basically support the information that I have been receiving from animal friends, angels, and other beings of light for a number of years.

They have asked that I share this information with others. The following communication was given to me by a council consisting of every species of animal as well as plants, rocks, waters, and other living forms. They spoke to me with one voice.

"Just as a plant grows toward the light, so do all other forms of life. There are those who can resist the light from a place of fear—the fear of losing their individuality, the fear of shattering the lie that they are separate from others. Yet the soul always knows the truth. If one becomes quiet and journeys into the heart, this is where truth lives.

"The energies from planets and stars, from the cosmos are affecting the Earth. And the Earth is affecting the cosmos. Doors of light are opening.

"Do you think only humans are a part of this evolutionary shift? No, it's every living form. We are all part of the whole. Remember.

"The Earth breathes, the plants breathe, the rivers breathe, the animals breathe, the humans breathe, the sky breathes. All beings are interconnected. The life force and intelligence flows through all life forms.

"We are helping to heal Earth. Recall the wonderment of all living forms. All are of equal value and to be loved.

"We are a part of Earth's soul, which is an aspect of the Creator's soul of the whole. Let go of the old lies that have led you astray. See the truth that there is only light and love. Be at peace. Trust. Earth is a beautiful planet. Don't fear growth. Go with love's flow.

"You ask, how can you help? Pray and meditate. Be joyful. Send yourselves, the Earth, and all other living forms love and light. Every being is helping to create and assist with this transformation.

"We pray and meditate. We vibrate in frequencies that most humans cannot hear right now, but many will come to hear our voices. These frequencies are raising the vibrations of all. Animals know how to live and express from the heart. Don't get caught in outer appearances. Trust your heart.

"The Earth's core and aura is transforming into light and love. Many dimensional doors are opening. This can be difficult since you are in physical form. Yet the physical is being transmuted, too. We are all becoming our true selves as we return to love, light, joy. Our souls dance in celebration."

THE WHALES COMMUNICATED the following to me. Their message is very similar to that of the other animals, yet there are subtle differences in how they each present their messages. The whales' communications were songs that filled every cell in my body.

"We are emissaries of the light from far-away places and spaces. We were here long before humans. We helped introduce our energies to the Earth and continue to do so. Our species sees the bigger picture of what's going on.

"We deeply desire to help humans understand that there are many forms of communication. Ours is a language of song, of love, of light, of frequency.

"We are sad that humans have continued to disregard their higher Nature, not understanding what their thoughts and actions do in terms of affecting the Earth, those on the Earth, and all beings existing in and around the Earth and beyond.

"Our souls have chosen to live in physical forms that do not have hands and feet. We do not have any desire to control, but to love. We sing songs of creation from our souls.

"You cannot understand the way in which our brains and frequencies work. It is beyond scientific thought, and therefore, our way of being and our souls are not seen for who we truly are by most.

"We are sad that those of the Earth are not embracing us in a way that would benefit the whole, or we could say the All.

"We're not here to judge, but to teach and to guide humans into their souls' desire to evolve along with the Earth and every other living being in the cosmos.

"The human mind has a hard time expanding to understand the truth that we are all one, but the heart knows this is true. What you do unto others, you do unto yourselves. We are all Source.

"We have been speaking to those who we know would hear us. We are not afraid for our bodies to die, but are disconcerted by the choices humans have made in regard to their lives and this planet. Many of the life forms are here to teach, heal, and guide you. The Earth desires war, hate, and greed to end. We are here to show you that love is real. We're helping raise the frequencies of Earth with our songs. Humans seem to have the hardest time letting go of their patterns, even when they know they don't work. Open to love, joy, and oneness.

"We have chosen to live in the waters to show you that every essence, whether on land or sea or in the air, is important and of value.

"Many upheavals are happening with the Earth and this will continue. The Earth is being set free. We are radiating frequencies of light and love from the waters. Humans are and will be discovering other dimensions within themselves. We are assisting humans in knowing that they are wonderful beings who have forgotten who they are. Feel the love within, and put love into action. We who swim in the oceans know how to do this and do in our communities.

"Our hope is for humans to choose love over hate, greed, and control."

How Does Transition Affect Animals?

MANY PEOPLE CONTINUE to call and ask me about what's going on with their animals' sudden and odd, erratic behaviors. Animals are moving through the same changes that we are. I usually receive more calls in regard to this when I am experiencing major energetic shifts. The animals need support since they, too, are having trouble with imbalances due to continual alterations with energies.

PEOPLE AND ANIMALS around the world are experiencing symptoms due to higher frequencies flooding the Earth. As the old continues to be cleared, we're adjusting vibrationally and learning how to embrace all aspects of ourselves.

When there are sudden interdimensional shifts happening, I hear people say such things as: I think I'm losing it. This is weird, but my cat and dog and I all were sick today. I'm scattered and feel like I'm everywhere. I feel like I'm on a roller coaster. My dog growled at me, which he has never done. I'm depressed. I'm feeling dizzy and have headaches. I'm having trouble sleeping. I'm overly emotional. I'm having visions and dreams about the Earth. Animals are talking to me in my dreams. My goals seem unimportant to me. I feel like I'm falling apart. I want to go home to the light.

Some animals may have a challenging time staying grounded in their bodies. Some may feel ill, act more emotional, appear spacey, become aggressive, or suddenly start hiding in closets or other areas that feel safe. They may lose their footing or balance. This is because they're seeing and feeling what's happening with the Earth as well as the frequency changes. Most animals are very sensitive to these shifts. We know that animals pick up on a storm or earthquake before it hits.

A client called and told me that her cat Brad was acting disoriented and wanted me to check him out. When I did I found he was half out of his body, energetically speaking. I asked him what had happened. He communicated, "I'm having trouble staying in my body with all the transitions going on. I was in one dimension and suddenly found myself in a number of dimensions at once and was pulled partially out of my body." His guardian angels and I assisted him with getting back into his body and helped ground him, so he could continue his wonderful work here on Earth helping to bring in more light.

Animals and Interdimensional Travel

ANIMALS AND OTHER living forms are aware that they are multidimensional beings. They have the ability to move in and out of various dimensions and realities like

Brad. Yet this does not make them exempt from challenges since they inhabit physical form.

A woman called and said, "I was watching my cat sitting in the backyard. She got up and walked toward the fence, and as she jumped up, her paws never touched the fence. She disappeared and a second later was sitting in my neighbor's backyard."

One night I was gazing at a full moon. I glanced over at my neighbor's roof, and there was a big raccoon scampering across the shingles. I rubbed my eyes and looked again to make sure I wasn't imagining this. The raccoon was still there. Then the raccoon simply vanished, and within a few seconds I heard the scurry of paws on my roof, directly above me. The raccoon had transported over to my roof by traveling interdimensionally.

With all the shifts going on, the animals and we humans are often experiencing more than one dimension at a time. (This can be happening even though we may not be consciously aware of it.) This might cause disorientation and confusion to our bodies and minds. The body and mind can have a tough time knowing what to do with all this. This is why it's paramount to remember to breathe and ground as we walk through these exciting changes. It's equally important to take time to let your animal friend and yourself connect with Nature on a regular basis. This will help a great deal.

Balancing Energies

PEOPLE CALL ME FOR HELP when they intuit that their animal friend is having a difficult time dealing with transitional energies. Some animals exhibit behavioral changes as I have mentioned.

Many animals like Brad communicate to me if they are having trouble staying grounded and aligned because of the shifts going on.

Initially, Beth's feline Serenity, whose essence is from another galaxy, showed me that her aura's energies were scattered and asked me to assist in re-aligning them. She then requested that I help balance her recently activated chakras, which exist in different dimensions. After all of this was done, she opened fully to her multidimensional selves and continues to do her work here on Earth in a much bigger way.

Serenity talked with me. "I am Rainbow. I am helping to clear away the old and bring in the new. I live in this body and beyond. My group soul is helping to raise the Earth's frequencies. We are all here to help each other. Hold to the light. All is in divine order. Hearts are opening."

This experience with Serenity opened the door for me to begin assisting animals with balancing and integrating the higher frequencies with their chakra systems, auras, multidimensional selves, and light bodies.

After doing this work, Serenity's person noticed a big difference in her aura and actions in very positive ways.

Dorothy's dog Larry asked me to help balance his chakra system. So I did but I could see other chakra centers, which had been dormant, starting to become activated. Right away, the angels told me to let them open naturally, which I would have done anyway. But when Larry and I communicated several months later, he asked if I would help balance and align the newly opened chakras with the rest of his energy system, which I proceeded to do. When I talked with his person later, he said that Larry was now more grounded and happier.

A man called me about his parrot Samantha. She and I had communicated several times during previous consults. Samantha is a delightful, high-energy being. She showed me bright rainbows flashing all around her. She wanted me to see and understand that she was "Rainbow," like Serenity. She communicated messages that she, and others with wings, are helping balance the Earth's vibrations.

Samantha has only been in her parrot body about a year, and has come in to do her part with transition. She is a highly evolved being in tune with her multidimensional selves. Yet, with the energies constantly reorganizing, sometimes Samantha needs adjustments with moving into a better sense of balance and alignment to help her do her work more comfortably; kind of like a tuneup.

After communicating with Serenity, Larry, and Samantha, I now refer to the highly evolved beings who are here to help bring in transition, whether they be animal, human or other, as "Rainbows."

Clearing Away Old Boundaries

As frequencies continue to shift, especially since the earthquake and tsunami, the animals are keenly aware of the density, or old patterns, that are being cleansed from the Earth. The Earth, humans, and other living forms are experiencing boundary changes in healthy ways. All of us are being asked to let go of old pains and to forgive, which enables us to become more open to ourselves and others. Eventually, old arbitrary boundaries will dissolve and we'll ultimately return to oneness again. Yet, each individual will progress at his own pace.

One woman called to tell me that she had seen a hawk sitting beside a squirrel on a picnic table, more than once, in her backyard. I am hearing stories about how animals who don't usually get close physically to humans are now doing so. On the Discovery Channel they showed a lioness mothering a fawn who had lost her mother. This isn't far off from a lion lying beside a lamb. A report from Nairobi told about a baby hippo who survived the tsunami and who has now formed a bond with a male, century-old tortoise in an animal facility in Mombassa. They eat and sleep together. There are many stories like these that I continue to find out about.

Also, animals are appearing in places where they've never appeared before. As I mentioned at the beginning of this chapter, birds are migrating to different locations now. One might say this could be due to loss of habitat, but there are too many instances of this now happening with various species.

The changes in the magnetic fields are confusing many animals. As some animals move in and out of various dimensions spontaneously they can become disoriented. This can cause some strange behaviors, as mentioned earlier.

One night while watching the news there was a story about a deer, not far from where I live, who jumped through a patio window and attacked a man. His wife called the police. When the police arrived they had to pull the deer off the man. The man was hospitalized for several days. This deer had lost her way.

When I perform soul recovery work, or communicate with an animal who has crossed over, I see and encounter other realms. I see Nature spirits, angels, and other beings who are present to help and who are doing their work. With major shifts happening, they continue to tell me that they are having to adjust to the many interdimensional shifts, too.

A Higher Order of Beings

I HAVE BEEN WORKING WITH animals and children who are very gifted psychically. Many of these souls are angels, star beings, and other beings who have traveled from other worlds and galaxies to assist with the ongoing transitions. They are raising the Earth's vibrations. As mentioned earlier, I refer to these beings as Rainbows, whether they be in an animal or human body.

Remember, there is no difference between a soul that resides in a human versus a cat body. Soul is soul. I only differentiate between humans and animals for the sake of clarity.

Experiencing the Shifts

PEOPLE ASK ME WHAT kind of changes we will experience as the Earth continues to throw off old densities and shift into the higher frequency of love and light. Some are obvious, such as the recent earthquakes, tsunamis, and floods. Other changes will continue to occur with land shifting and global climate alterations. These are ways in which the Earth can release the old and begin to renew or transmute herself.

Eastern Asia

ABOUT THREE WEEKS BEFORE the earthquake and tsunami in Eastern Asia I had been getting bad headaches and feeling dizzy but didn't know why. When the quake and tsunami hit, I understood. I experienced headaches off and on for weeks after the disaster. I still get headaches when there are numerous changes going on within and around the Earth. There are many nights when I receive visions of the dimensional shifts. The Earth is in a constant state of rebalancing. Not only did this event alter the planet's rotation, but it decreased the length of our day. Also, it slightly changed the planet's shape and shifted the North Pole by a number of centimeters. Our moon's orbiting pattern was also affected. The frequencies of the sun, Earth, and moon are now different. These changes, and others yet to come, are aligning our entire solar system in a whole new way.

A number of clients told me that their animal companions were suddenly experiencing physical pain, having seizures, or acting aggressive before, during, and after the quake and tsunami. Animals feel and react to whatever is going on around and within the Earth. We do too, but often aren't aware of it. The animals and we are, on various levels, trying to re-align our energy fields with the the higher frequencies and energy shifts.

I communicated with animals in eastern Asia after the quake and tsunami. A council of animals spoke with one voice. "We knew what was coming. Many of us moved to higher ground if we could. We are acutely aware of all the shifts that are taking place within and around Mother Earth. We understand that these changes must take place, and we are doing our best to help sustain the energetic balances of the Earth along with the many beings of light from other galaxies and realms.

"Although many people and animals shed their physical bodies during this huge dimensional opening, many of them are now helping from the other side. Others have already re-entered the Earth's plane to assist with upcoming climate and geomagnetic shifts with the Earth.

"Our souls are helping humans to come to a place of surrender so they can accept the upcoming positive changes in the evolutionary process. We are all One.

"Love is always the key. During this disaster, many humans turned to one another and to the divine love within themselves.

"A number of veils lifted as density dropped away. Mother Earth emerged further into the higher frequencies and dimensions of love and light in a new way. A birthing process. Do not be afraid but rejoice for all is as it should be. Remember, the Earth's soul is evolving as is every soul. All of creation is evolving into love."

The animals are always trying to lead and protect us, but many experienced this firsthand with this disaster. After the tsunami was over, elephants in Thailand came down a hill and picked up children with their trunks. Then they ran back up the hill. When the children were safe on the hill, the elephants came back down and led the adults up the hill. There are other stories people have told about how animals helped or saved them.

Every living being is and will experience these changes in his or her own way. How you experience the ongoing transformation will depend on your perceptions about who you are, what your life is like, what you think reality is, and what you think the Creator is. What are you willing to let go of so you can open up to the new you?

As the new paradigm continues to take shape, all living beings have the opportunity to allow more light into their bodies and lives. As we become more light, all of us will vibrate into higher dimensions that we are ready to embrace. Again, this doesn't mean that Earth will no longer exist, but she will not exist in the same way. We're moving away from struggle and focusing on peace and harmony. The key is to surrender and to go with the flow.

This is a wonderful time to be alive. Let's celebrate our return to love.

Let us see through the illusion of the third dimension, which is the misconception that we are separate from one another and from the Source which has manifested all of creation.

Supporting One Another

THE REASON FOR SHARING this information, once again, is for us to be aware of how these changes affect not only us but our beloved animal companions. Taking time to be with our animal companions and in Nature reminds us what's important.

If we set our intention for love and healing, we are actively participating in assisting with these cosmic shifts. As humankind becomes more conscious and balanced, this allows more light and love to enter our lives, which helps to heal all.

Let us be aware that our animal friends need more support than ever before. Chapter Ten, Understanding and Supporting the Animals We Love, offers plenty of suggestions and ways to give our animal companions support during these ongoing changes.

Grounding Technique to Help Your Animal Companions

Gently place your hand on your animal friend's shoulder. Move your hand slowly down his leg until you reach his paw. Hold your hand over his paw for a few seconds and take a deep breath. Remove your hand. (Do not run your hand up the leg because this ungrounds.) Move to the other shoulder and do the same motion. Then move your hand to his hip, doing the same downward motion. You can do this grounding technique with any animal. If the animal or being doesn't have legs, simply run your hand from the top of his body down to the ground. Please make sure you are grounded before you do this with an animal friend.

Doing Our Part—How Can We Help?

We can help by becoming more conscious in how we treat animals, Nature, each other, and other living forms.

We can send love and healing thoughts and images to the Earth, ourselves, and all life forms.

It's important to pay attention to our inner shifts. When we are centered and grounded we are supporting the whole. This gives us all a sense of peace. Let us remember to embrace and respect ourselves as well as all other living forms as we continue this journey.

Being in Nature lifts our spirit and helps us to maintain balance. It helps us to remember our connection with the Earth. We can bless the trees, rivers, the sky, and all living forms as we stroll through the woods. At night we can radiate love to the stars. We can pray, meditate, tone, sing, play a musical instrument, dance, laugh, along with everything else that celebrates life. Creative expression and beauty lifts our souls. Painting, writing poetry, gardening, playing with companion animals and children, or anything that gives joy raises our vibration, which contributes to global healing.

Let us listen to the quiet voice of the divine within. Let us actualize love and light.

The following is a simple but powerful visualization that my guardian angels shared with me over twenty years ago. You can do this individually or with a group. Sometimes, I close my workshops with this meditation. The only difference in doing this with a group is to visualize the Earth suspended in the center of the circle.

Earth Meditation

Sit in a comfortable position. Take a deep breath and ground. Imagine Mother Earth, about the size of a globe, suspended about three feet from your heart. Take another deep breath, and as you exhale, send her Universal love and light. Sometimes I send pink light, which is the color of love. See and feel her surrounded in this love and light.

Interspecies Communication

MORE PEOPLE ARE ACCEPTING interspecies communication as real, and want to learn how to communicate with animals nonverbally. This is an important key to opening the doors that will guide humankind into remembering that all of life is sacred and that we're all one.

As new frequencies of light splash onto the Earth, we can choose to let our hearts open like spring flowers. Communicating with animals is a heart-to-heart language. In remembering that we can and already know how to communicate with animals and Nature, we are finding our way home to Eden, or returning to love. In a way, we are returning to or evolving into our original DNA blueprint, which did not include ego. Yet ego will transform as we ultimately transform into light and love. We are being set free to move beyond the mind's limiting thoughts about who we are, what reality is, and what is possible. The truth is that all things are possible.

As we continue to evolve, we will once again communicate silently with all life forms, and know each other as ourselves.

Even though this process can be challenging, remember it's all good. We are learning how to be unconditional love. The animals understand this and are guiding us in opening our hearts. What a great gift!

The following poem shows how other living beings can open and help us to remember what bright souls we are. These words poured out of me after having a deeply moving encounter with a newly born praying mantis.

The Visitor

Several flies flew by, but I didn't spot
you until an hour later
as I sat comfy in my chair
beside the ivy, writing
under pink cloudy light.
Looking up, there you were,
newly emerged praying
mantis about half the size of my thumb
ambling in a pool of leaves
on thread thin legs.

Your slender body
green as spring decorated with silk
woven wings astounded me. So perfect,
in your coming to live a life
on this Earth.

Aren't you beautiful, I cooed.
Turning your tiny, heart-shaped
head, you gazed
into my eyes with those
unmistakable mantis eyes,

no hint of fear, as if you
were larger than me, as if
we had known each other
for centuries.
And we both knew we had.

My instinct was to be still
and bow. We talked
in a holy green glow only
we understood,
you moving me beyond myself.

Then I placed you among
luscious evergreens, and watched
you blend into the peaceful
green green
praying for the world.

Jacquelin Smith has experienced tremendous love and respect for all living forms since early childhood. Since 1972 she has been actively involved in studying animal life and behavior. She is a leader in the field of telepathic communication with animals.

After receiving a B.A., Jacquelin worked as a licensed animal technician and dog trainer while studying psychology.

She has communicated with animals in zoological parks as well as in the wild during her travels in Africa and South America. She has sat among mountain gorillas and walked among tortoises on the Galapagos Islands.

Jacquelin felt that if telepathic communication can exist person-to-person, why not person-to-animal? Since 1979, she has focused on telepathic communication with both domestic and exotic animals. She combines holistic and traditional techniques to help solve issues.

In 1998 she created The Divine Prayer Line For Animals.

Jacquelin lectures, teaches workshops, and offers private consultations.

Her animal communication work continues to receive media coverage through radio interviews and television talk shows.

Jacquelin has communicated nationally and internationally with thousands of individuals about their animal companions.

To Contact Jacquelin

Jacquelin is available for lectures, workshops, and private consultations. For information about her workshops, the prayer line, this book, and audiotapes, you can visit her website at *www.jacquelinsmith.com* or email her at:

jacquelinsmith@jacquelinsmith.com

To order additional copies of this book,
please send full amount plus $5.00 for
postage and handling for the first book and
$1.00 for each additional book.

Send orders to:

Galde Press, Inc.
PO Box 460
Lakeville, Minnesota 55044-0460

Credit card orders call 1–800–777–3454
Phone (952) 891–5991 • Fax (952) 891–6091
Visit our website at http://www.galdepress.com

Write for our free catalog.